CANADIAN HEROES SERIES

THE STORY OF ISAAC BROCK

"The Story of Isaac Brock"
is the first volume of the
"Canadian Heroes Series"
for children, published under
the auspices of the Ontario
Library Association, and
recommended by the In-
spector of Public Libraries.

TO BE FOLLOWED BY OTHER VOLUMES

THE STORY OF

ISAAC BROCK

HERO, DEFENDER AND SAVIOUR OF
UPPER CANADA
1812

BY

WALTER R. NURSEY

" By his unrivalled skill, by great
And veteran service to the state,
By worth adored,
He stood, in high dignity,
The proudest knight of chivalry,
Knight of the Sword."
—*Coplas de Manrique.*

TORONTO :
WILLIAM BRIGGS
1908

Upper Canada Press

an imprint of

American History Press
Franklin, Tennessee
(888) 521-1789
Visit us on the Internet at:
www.Americanhistorypress.com

ISBN 13: 978-0-9830827-2-9
Library of Congress Control Number: 2011928180

First Edition May 2011

Printed in the United States of America on acid-free
paper. This book meets all ANSI standards for
archival quality.

A WORD TO THE READER

THAT Isaac Brock is entitled to rank as the foremost defender of the flag Western Canada has ever seen, is a statement which no one familiar with history can deny. Brock fought and won out when the odds were all against him.

At a time when almost every British soldier was busy fighting Napoleon in Europe, upon General Brock fell the responsibility of upholding Britain's honour in America. He was " the man behind the gun "—the undismayed man—when the integrity of British America was threatened by a determined enemy.

His success can be measured by the fact that it is only since the war of 1812-14 that the British flag has been properly respected in the western hemisphere. It is also a fact that after the capture of Detroit the Union Jack became more firmly rooted in the affections of the Canadian people than ever.

It must not be forgotten that the capture of this stronghold was almost as far-reaching in its ultimate effect as the victory of Wolfe on the Plains of Abraham, and was fraught with little, if any, less import to Canada.

A Word to the Reader

What with the timidity of Prevost, and the tactical blunders of both himself and Sheaffe, the immediate influence upon the enemy of the victories at Detroit and Queenston was almost nullified. Had Brock survived Queenston, or even had his fixed, militant policy been allowed to prevail from the first, it is safe to say there would have been no armistice, no placating of a clever, intriguing foe, and no two years' prolongation of the war. Had the capitulation of Detroit, the crushing defeat at Queenston, and the wholesale desertion of Wadsworth's cowardly legions at Lewiston, been followed up by the British with relentless assault "all along the line"— before the enemy had time to recover his grip—then our hero's feasible plan, which he had pleaded with Prevost to permit, namely, to sweep the Niagara frontier and destroy Sackett's Harbor—the key to American naval supremacy of the lakes—could, there is no good reason to doubt, have been carried out. The purpose of this little book is not, however, to deal in surmises.

The story of Sir Isaac Brock's life should convey to the youth of Canada a significance similar to that which the bugle-call of the trumpeter, sounding the advance, conveys to the soldier in the ranks. Reiteration of Brock's deeds should help to develop a better appreciation of his work, a truer conception of his heroism, a wiser understanding of his sacrifice.

Many a famous man owes a debt of inspiration to some

A Word to the Reader

other great life that went before him. Not until every boy
in Canada is thoroughly familiar with " Master Isaac's "
achievements will he be qualified to exclaim with the
Indian warrior, Tecumseh,

" THIS IS A MAN."

W. R. N.

Toronto, October, 1908.

NOTE.—Of the hundred and more books and documents con-
sulted in a search for facts I would register my special obligations to Tupper's " Life of Brock "; Auchinleck's " History of
the War of 1812-14 "; Cruikshank's " Documentary History," and
Richardson's " War of 1812 " (edited by Casselman).

CONTENTS

vii

Contents

LIST OF ILLUSTRATIONS

NOTE.—For full description of above illustrations, see Appendix, page 175.

Introduction

The original copy for this book was written less than a century after Brock's death, and it has now been almost two hundred years since that historic event. Yet the story revealed between these covers is as memorable and significant today as it was when the incidents of his life occurred. Both children and adults still love hearing the story of General Brock and Chief Tecumseh, and while this narrative was originally intended for a younger ear, a glimpse into its contents will quickly reveal its universal appeal to readers of all ages.

As the Canadian government anticipates a great influx of visitors to celebrate the 200th anniversary of the War of 1812, many of the sites mentioned in this book are being given a physical upgrade and fresh interpretation. This would be an ideal time to make an effort to visit as many of them as you can in order to experience the benefits of history first hand. Knowledge of Canadian history is vital to the enjoyment of the country that we all share, and adds to the enrichment of life in general.

Travel to Amherstburg and stand at the spot where Brock and Tecumseh met for the first time (page 96 "This is a MAN"). Visit the former location of Fort Detroit, explore its grounds and imagine them during the time of Tecumseh and Brock. Relax on the porch at the Bâby mansion in Sandwich, which is now an historic site, and walk in the footsteps of Generals Brock, Harrison, Hull and Colonel Proctor, recalling at the same time the feats of Chiefs Tecumseh, Pontiac, and Splitlog, who also walked its halls. Venture to Queenston Heights and pay tribute to General Hall at Brock's Monument (page 174), or travel over the same road where "Brock's Midnight Gallop" took place (page 135).

In Windsor, Ontario you can visit both of the Bâby mansions, and continue on to the well-preserved site of Fort Malden in the picturesque town of Amherstburg. Afterwards cross the river into the state of Michigan and visit the site of Fort Detroit and the Raisin River Battle (page 93) while discovering Spring Wells (page 105), now the site of Fort Wayne. Head over to the Niagara frontier and imagine the struggles that Brock experienced just before he died protecting our country.

I hope that you enjoy the story of General Brock, and the battles he fought while defending Canada. One of the many lessons to be learned from the book is that if one reads, lives and walks in our history, taking the time to explore the battlefields, forts and sites mentioned, a rich world will be discovered in the process. This is what makes the study of the past both fun and rewarding.

Chris Carter
Author and Historian
Spring 2011

[Note: For more information about the historic Bâby Mansion read *Souvenirs of the Past* by William Baby].

"ST. PETER'S PORT, GUERNSEY, 18×6."

THE STORY OF ISAAC BROCK

CHAPTER I.

OUR HERO'S HOME—GUERNSEY.

OFF the coast of Brittany, where the Bay of Biscay fights the white horses of the North Sea, the Island of Guernsey rides at anchor. Its black and yellow, red and purple coast-line, summer and winter, is awash with surf, burying the protecting reefs in a smother of foam. Between these drowned ridges of despair, which warn the toilers of the sea of an intention to engulf them, tongues of ocean pierce the grim chasms of the cliffs.

Between this and the sister island of Alderney the teeth of the Casquets cradle the skeleton of many a stout ship, while above the level of the sea the amethyst peaks of Sark rise like phantom bergs. In the sunlight the rainbow-coloured slopes of Le Gouffre jut upwards a jumble of glory. Exposed to the full fury of an Atlantic gale, these islands are well-nigh obliterated in drench. From where the red gables cluster on the heights of Fort George, which overhang the harbour, to the thickets of Jerbourg, valley and plain, at the time we write of, were a gorgeous carpet of anemones, daffodils, primroses and poppies.

These are tumultuous latitudes. Sudden hurricanes,

The Story of Isaac Brock

with the concentrated force of the German Ocean behind them, soon scourge the sea into a whirlpool and extinguish every landmark in a pall of gray. For centuries tumult and action have been other names for the Channel Islands. It is no wonder that the inhabitants partake of the nature of their surroundings. Contact with the elements produces a love for combat. As this little book is largely a record of strife, and of one of Guernsey's greatest fighting sons, it may be well to recall the efforts that preceded the birth of our hero and influenced his career, and through which Guernsey retained its liberties.

For centuries Guernsey had been whipped into strife. From the raid upon her independence by David Bruce, the exiled King of Scotland, early in 1300, on through the centuries up to the seventeenth, piping times of peace were few and far between. The resources of the island led to frequent invasions from France, but while fighting and resistance did not impair the loyalty of the islanders, it nourished a love of freedom, and of hostility to any enemy who had the effrontery to assail it. As a rule the sojourn of these invaders was brief. When sore pressed in a pitched battle on the plateau above St. Peter's Port, the inhabitants would retreat behind the buttresses of Castle Cornet, when, as in the invasion by Charles V. of France, the fortress proving impregnable, the besiegers would collect their belongings and sail away.

In the fourteenth century Henry VI. of England, in consideration of a red rose as annual rental, conveyed the entire group to the Duke of Warwick. But strange privileges were from time to time extended to these audacious people. Queen Elizabeth proclaimed the islands a world's

Our Hero's Home

sanctuary, and threw open the ports as free harbours of refuge in time of war. She authorized protection to " a distance on the ocean as far as the eye of man could reach." This act of grace was cancelled by George the Third, who regarded it as a premium on piracy. In Cromwell's time Admiral Blake had been instructed to raise the siege of Castle Cornet. He brought its commander to his senses, but only after nine years of assault, and not before 30,000 cannon-balls had been hurled into the town.

Late in the fourteenth century, when the English were driven out of France, not a few of those deported, who had the fighting propensity well developed, made haste for the Channel Islands, where rare chances offered to handle an arquebus for the King. Among those who sought refuge in Guernsey there landed, not far from the Lion's Rock at Cobo, an English knight, Sir Hugh Brock, lately the keeper of the Castle of Derval in Brittany, a man " stout of figure and valiant of heart." This harbour of refuge was St. Peter's Port.

> "Within a long recess there lies a bay,
> An island shades it from the rolling sea,
> And forms a port."

The islet that broke the Atlantic rollers was Castle Cornet. Sir Hugh Brock, or Badger in the ancient Saxon time—an apt name for a tenacious fighter—shook hands with fate. He espied the rocky cape of St. Jerbourg, and ofttimes from its summit he would shape bold plans for the future, the maturing of which meant much to those of his race destined to follow.

The commercial growth of the Channel Islands has been

13

The Story of Isaac Brock

divided into five periods, those of fishing, knitting (the age of the garments known as "jerseys" and "guernseys"), privateering, smuggling, and agriculture and commerce. To the third period belong these records. The prosperity of the islands was greatest from the middle of the seventeenth century up to the overthrow of Napoleon at Waterloo and the close of Canada's successful fight against invasion in 1815. During this period the building of ships for the North Atlantic and Newfoundland trade opened new highways for commerce, but the greatest factor in this development was the " reputable business " of privateering, which must not be confounded either with buccaneering or yard-arm piracy. It was only permitted under regular letters of marque, was ranked as an honorable occupation, and those bold spirits, the wild " beggars of the sea "—who preferred the cutlass and a roving commission in high latitudes to ploughing up the cowslips in the Guernsey valleys, or knitting striped shirts at home—were recognized as good fighting men and acceptable enemies.

Trade in the islands, consequent upon the smuggling that followed and the building of many ships, produced much wealth, creating a class of newly rich and with it some " social disruption."

Notable in the " exclusive set," not only on account of his athletic figure and handsome face, but for his winning manners and ability to dance, though but a boy, was Isaac Brock. Isaac—a distant descendant of bold Sir Hugh —was the eighth son of John Brock, formerly a midshipman in the Royal Navy, a man of much talent and, like his son, of great activity. Brock, the father, did

14

Our Hero's Home

not enjoy the fruit of his industry long, for in 1777, in his 49th year, he died in Brittany, leaving a family of fourteen children. Of ten sons, Isaac, destined to become "the hero and defender of Upper Canada," was then a flaxen-haired boy of eight.

Anno Domini 1769 will remain a memorable one in the history of the empire. Napoleon, the conqueror of Europe, and Wellington, the conqueror of Napoleon, were both sons of 1769. This same year Elizabeth de Lisle, wife of John Brock, of St. Peter's Port, bore him his eighth son, the Isaac referred to, also ordained to become "a man of destiny." Isaac's future domain was that greater, though then but little known, dominion beyond the seas, Canada—a territory of imperial extent, whose resources at that time came within the range of few men's understanding. Isaac Brock, as has been shown, came of good fighting stock, was of clean repute and connected with most of the families of high degree on the Island. The de Beauvoirs, Saumarez, de Lisles, Le Marchants, Careys, Tuppers and many others distinguished in arms or diplomacy, were his kith and kin. His mind saturated with the stories of the deeds of his ancestors, and possessed of a spirit of adventure developed by constant contact with soldiers and sailors, it was but natural that he became cast in a fighting mould and that "to be a soldier" was the height of his ambition.

Perhaps Isaac Brock's chief charm, which he retained in a marked degree in after life—apart from his wonderful thews and sinews, his stature and athletic skill—was his extreme modesty and gentleness. The fine old maxim of the child being "father to the man" in his case held good.

The Story of Isaac Brock

CHAPTER II.

SCHOOL AND PASTIMES.

GUERNSEY abounded in the natural attractions that are dear to the youth of robust body and adventurous nature. Isaac, though he excelled in field sports and was the admiration of his school-fellows, was sufficiently strong within himself to find profit in his own society. In the thickets that overlooked Houmet Bay he found solace apart from his companions. There he would recall the stories told him of the prowess of his ancestor, William de Beauvoir, that man of great courage, a Jurat of the royal court. Even here he did not always escape intruders. Outside the harbour of St. Peter's Port, separated by an arm of the sea, rose the Ortach Rock, between the Casquets and " Aurigny's Isle," a haunted spot, once the abode of a sorcerer named Jochmus. To secure quiet he would frequently visit this isolated place, in spite of the resident devil, the devil-fish, or the devil-strip of treacherous water which ran between.

He was not ten when, to the amazement of his friends, in imitation of Leander but without the same inducements, he swam the half mile to the reefs of Castle Cornet and back again, through a boiling sea and rip-tides that ran like mill-races. This performance he repeated again and again. For milder amusement he would tramp to the water-lane that stole through the Moulin Huet, a bower of red roses and perfume, or walk by moonlight to

School and Pastimes

the mystic cromlechs, where the early pagans and the warlocks and witches of later days flitted round the ruined altars.

Though Isaac was self-contained and resolute he had a restless spirit. Fearless, without a touch of the braggart, his courage was of the valiant order, the quality that accompanies a lofty soul in a strong body. For his constant courtesy and habit of making sacrifices for his friends, he was in danger of being canonized by his schoolfellows.

About this time, shortly after his father's death, it was suggested he should leave the Queen Elizabeth School on the Island and study at Southampton. Here he tried his best, boy though he was, to live up to the standard of what he had been told were his obligations as a gentleman, acquiring, too, a little book-learning and much every-day knowledge.

Isaac's holidays, always spent in his beloved Guernsey, increased the thirst for adventure. The spirit of conquest, the controlling influence of his after life, grew upon him. Something accomplished, something done, was the daily rule. To scale an impossible cliff with the wings of circling sea-fowl beating in his face, to land a big conger eel without receiving a shock, to rescue a partridge from a falcon, to shoot a rabbit at fifty paces, to break a wild pony, or even to scan a complicated line in his syntax—these were achievements, small perhaps, but typical of his desire. His young soul was stirred; the blood coursed in his veins as the sap courses in the trees of the forest in spring; his mind, susceptible to the influences of nature, was strengthened and purified by these pursuits.

17

The Story of Isaac Brock

In the shelter of silent trossach, on wind-swept height, or on wildest, ever-restless sea, he would, as the mood seized him, take his solitary outings. These jaunts, he told his mother, gave him time to reflect and resolve. It was not strange that he selected a profession that presented the opportunities he craved.

.   .   .   .

England with folded arms was at peace. The Treaty of Versailles had terminated the disastrous war with America. The independence of the "Thirteen States" had been recognized. The world was drawing a long breath, filling its fighting lungs, awaiting the death struggle with Napoleon for the supremacy of Europe. Yet the spirit of war lingered in the air. It even drifted on the breeze across the Channel to Guernsey, and filtered through the trees that crowned the Lion's Rock at Cobo. It invaded the valleys of the Petit Bot and stirred the bulrushes in the marshes of Havelet. The pulse of our hero throbbed with the subtle infection. Not with the brute lust for other men's blood, but with the instinct of the true patriot to shed, if need be, his own blood to maintain the right. He would follow the example of his ancestors and fight and die, if duty called him, in defence of king and country.

The sweet arrogance of youth uplifted him. Earth, air and water conspired to encourage him. To satisfy this unspoken craving for action he would, from his outlook on the Jerbourg crags—where bold Sir Hugh had sat for just such purpose years before—watch the Weymouth luggers making bad weather of it beyond the Casquets;

School and Pastimes

or challenge in his own boat the rip-tides between Sark
and Brechou, and the combers that romped between St.
Sampson and the Isle of Herm.

There was no limit to this boy's hardihood and daring.
The more furious the gale the more congenial the task.
Returning from these frequent baptisms of salt water, his
Saxon fairness and Norman freshness aglow with spray,
he would loiter on the beach to talk to the kelp gatherers
raking amid the breakers, and to watch the mackerel boats,
reefed down, flying to the harbour for shelter. The cray-
fish in the pools would tempt him, he would try his hand
at sand-eeling, or watch the surf men feed a devil-fish to
the crabs. Then up the gray benches of the furrowed
cliffs, starred with silver lichens and stone-crop, to where
ploughmen were leaving glistening furrows in the big
parsnip fields. Then on through the tangle of sweet-briar,
honeysuckle and wild roses, where birds nested in the per-
fumed foliage, until, the summit reached, surrounded by
purple heather and golden gorse, he would look on the sea
below, with Sark, like a " basking whale, burning in the
sunset." Then he would hurry to tell his mother of the
day's exploits, retiring to dream of strange lands and
turbulent scenes, in which the roll of drums and roar of
cannon seemed never absent.

With his youthful mind possessed with the exploits of
the King's soldiers in Europe and America, and influenced
by his brother John's example—then captain in the 8th
Regiment of the line—Isaac pleaded successfully to enter
the army. To better prepare for this all-important step,
and to become proficient in French, a necessary accom-
plishment, it was arranged, though he was only fifteen, to

19

The Story of Isaac Brock

place him with a Protestant clergyman in Rotterdam for one year, to complete his education.

His vacations now were few; his visits to the Island flying ones. But the old life still fascinated him. His physique developed as the weeks flew by, and he became more and more a striking personality. This was doubly true, for while he remained the champion swimmer, he was also the best boxer of his class, besides excelling in every other manly sport. In tugs-of-war and " uprooting the gorse " he had no equals, but a sense of his educational deficiencies kept him at his books.

He had only passed his sixteenth birthday when, one wild March morning in 1785, he was handed an important-looking document. It was a parchment with the King's seal attached, his commission of ensign in the 8th Regiment. Isaac at once joined the regimental depot in England. It was evident that his lack of learning would prove a barrier to promotion. He found that much of the leisure hitherto devoted to athletic sports must be given to study. Behind " sported oak," while dust accumulated on boxing-glove and foil—neither the banter of his brother officers nor his love for athletics inducing him to break the resolution—he bent to his work with a fixity of purpose that augured well for his future.

In every man's life there are milestones. Isaac Brock's life may fairly be divided into five periods. When he crossed the threshold of his Guernsey home and donned the uniform of the King he passed his *first* milestone.

From Ensign to Colonel

CHAPTER III.

FROM ENSIGN TO COLONEL.

In every young man's career comes a time of probation. During this critical period that youth is wise who enters into a truce with his feelings. This is the period when influences for good or bad assert themselves—the parting of the ways. The sign-posts are painted in capitals.

When Brock buttoned his scarlet tunic and strapped his sword on his hip, as fine a specimen of a clean-bodied, clean-minded youth as ever trod the turnpike of life, he knew that he was at the cross-roads. The trail before him was well blazed, but straight or crooked, rough or smooth, valley or height, it mattered little so long as he kept nourished the bright light of purpose that burned steadily within him.

Five years of uneventful service, chiefly in England, passed by, and our hero was celebrating his coming of age. His only inheritance was health, hope and courage. While neither monk nor hermit, he had so far been as steadfast as the Pole Star in respect to his resolutions. He had allowed nothing to induce him to break the rules engraved on brass that he had himself imposed. His mind had broadened, his spirits ran high, his conscience told him that he was graduating in the world's university with honour. His love for athletics still continued. He had the thews of a gladiator, and in his Guernsey stockings stood six feet two inches. Add to this an honest counten-

The Story of Isaac Brock

ance, with much gentleness of manner and great determination, and you have a faithful picture of Isaac Brock.

Upon obtaining his lieutenancy he returned to Guernsey, raised an independent company, and exchanged into the 49th, the Royal Berkshires, then stationed in Barbadoes. He now found himself looking at life under new conditions. While the beauties of Barbadoes enchanted him, his duties as a soldier were disappointing. They were limited to drill, dress parade, guard mounting, the erection of new fortifications, and patrolling the coast for vessels carrying prohibited cargoes.

Under the terms of a treaty made at Paris in 1773, United States produce for British West Indian ports could only be carried by British subjects in British ships. Britain's men-of-war were also authorized to seize any vessel laden with produce for or from any French colony. Brock was a soldier, not a policeman, and coast-guard duties palled upon him. His great diversion was in calculating the probabilities of invasion by the French. In expectation of this, the refortifying of the island was in progress. The memory of Admiral d'Estaing's visit with his fleet from Toulon, and the capture of St. Vincent, sent a chill through the island. The great victory by the British Admiral Rodney, when he whipped a superior French fleet to a standstill, was yet to come. Bastions and earthworks grew during the night like mushrooms. While Brock chafed under restraint, he knew how to improve the opportunity.

Fishing, shooting sea-fowl, and exploring the interior on horseback, were Brock's chief pastimes. He became a fearless horseman. Mount Hillaby rose 1,200 feet above

From Ensign to Colonel

the Caribbean Sea. The very crest of its almost impossible pinnacle Brock is said to have ascended on horseback. Between Bridgetown, in Barbadoes, and Kingston, Jamaica, he divided his time, and though monotonous, his life in the Windward Islands was not wholly void of adventure.

Shortly after joining his regiment at Bridgetown our hero had his first affair of honour, an opportunity to display his courage under most trying conditions. A certain captain in the 49th was a confirmed duellist, with a reputation of being a dead shot at short range. Resting upon his evil record, this braggart had succeeded in terrorizing the garrison, and it was soon Brock's turn to be selected for insult. But Isaac could not be bullied or intimidated. He promptly challenged and was as promptly accepted.

The fateful morning arrived. In a lonely spot, palmsheltered, and within sight of the sea breaking upon the coral reefs, principals and seconds met. There was no question in Brock's mind as to his duty—the duello at that time was the recognized court of appeal. If its purpose as originally designed had at times been infamously abused, it was still the one and only arbiter through which insults had to be purged and from which, for the "officer and gentleman," there was no escape.

Now Isaac, who was several inches taller and much bulkier than the scoundrel who had insulted him, declined to become a shining mark at the regulation twelve paces. He demanded from his fire-eating antagonist that the duel proceed on equal terms. Whipping out his kerchief, cool as a cucumber, his blue eyes steady and resolute, he insisted that *they both fire across it.* The fairness of the proposal

23

The Story of Isaac Brock

staggered the bully. The chances were not sufficiently one-sided. If this plan was acted upon he might himself be killed. He refused to comply. The code of honour and garrison approval sustained Brock in his contention, and the refusal of the professional killer to fight under even chances was registered in the mess-room as the act of a coward, and he left the regiment by compulsion.

In Jamaica the continued strain of inactivity under which our hero fretted told upon him, and he was struck down with fever, his cousin, Henry Brock, lieutenant in the 13th Foot, dying in Kingston of the same pestilence. At this time Isaac had as servant a soldier named Dobson, one of those faithful souls who, true as steel, once installed in their master's affection, remain loyal to the end. To the untiring attentions of this man Brock owed his life. Deep and mutual respect followed, and the two became inseparable. Where Brock went, there was Dobson, sharing his fortune and all the hard knocks of his military campaigns, a fellowship ending only with Dobson's death, shortly before his "beloved master" gave up his life on Queenston Heights.

Tropical malaria is hard to shake off. Release from duty was imperative, and as England was now calling for recruits, the War Office summoned Brock, an alluring sample of a soldier, to whom was assigned the task of licking the fighting country bumpkin—the raw material —into shape. This he did, first in England, then in Guernsey and Jersey. A vision of our hero, glorious in his uniform, was in itself sufficient to ensnare the senses of any country yokel. It was a militant age.

When quartered in Guernsey, and from the same heights

From Ensign to Colonel

of Jerbourg where but a few years before he was wont to sweep the ocean for belated fishing smacks, Brock saw his kinsman, Sir James Saumarez, and the white canvas of a small squadron, heave in sight from Plymouth Roads. The British sailor had been ordered to ascertain the strength of the French fleet. Saumarez' ships were far slower than those of the enemy, so, feigning the greatest desire to fight, he lured his opponent by a clever ruse. First he closed with him, and then, when his own capture seemed inevitable, hauled his wind, slipped through a maze of reefs by an intricate passage—long familiar to our hero—and found safety off La Vazon, where the Frenchmen dare not follow.

In June, 1795, Brock purchased his majority, but retained his command of the recruits. From toes to finger-tips Isaac was a soldier, bent on mastering every detail of the profession of his choice. A year after the return of the 49th to England, on the completion of his 28th year, he became by purchase senior lieutenant-colonel of his regiment. High honour and rapid promotion, considering that for five out of seven years' service he had remained an ensign. He had learned to recognize opportunity, the earthly captain of a man's fate.

> " For every day I stand outside your door,
>   And bid you wake and rise to fight and win."

But Brock's position was no sinecure. The regiment was in a badly demoralized condition. The laxity of the late commanding officer had created a deplorable state of things. To restore the lost *morale* of the corps was his first duty.

25

The Story of Isaac Brock

The thoroughness of his reforms can be best understood by quoting the words of the Duke of York, who declared that " out of one of the worst regiments in the service Colonel Brock had made the 49th one of the best."

From the Commander-in-Chief of a nation's army to a colonel—not yet thirty—of a marching regiment, this was an exceptional tribute.

Isaac's persistent endeavours were rapidly bringing their own reward.

NAVY HALL, REMNANT OF THE OLD "RED BARRACKS," NIAGARA, 1797.

Egmont-op-Zee and Copenhagen

CHAPTER IV.

EGMONT-OP-ZEE AND COPENHAGEN.

MEANWHILE the war cloud in Europe was growing apace. Holland had been forced into an alliance with France. War, no longer a spectre, but a grim monster, stalked the Continent. Everywhere the hostile arts of Bonaparte were rousing the nations. The breezes that had stirred the marshes of Havelet and awakened in Brock a sense of impending danger, now a furious gale, swept the empires. The roll of drums and roar of cannon that Isaac had listened to in his boyhood dreams were now challenging in deadly earnest. The great *reveille* that was awakening the world was followed by the British buglers calling to arms the soldiers of the King.

Notwithstanding the aversion of the English prime minister, Pitt, to commence hostilities, war was unavoidable. One of the twelve battalions of infantry selected for the front was the 49th. When the orders were read for the regiment to join the expedition to Holland, wild excitement prevailed in barracks. Active service had come at last. The parting of Brock with his family was softened by maternal pride in his appearance.

The tunic of the 49th was scarlet, with short swallowtails. The rolling lapels were faced with green, the coat being laced with white, with a high collar. The shako, which was originally surmounted by white feathers with black tips, a distinction for services in the American war

The Story of Isaac Brock

of 1776, at Bunker's Hill and Brandywine, was, at Brock's special request, replaced by a black plume. The officers wore their hair turned up behind and fastened with a black " flash." The spectacle of Master Isaac thus arrayed, in all the glory of epaulets and sabretache and the gold braid of a full colonel, reconciled the inhabitants of St. Peter's Port to his departure.

By the end of August the first division of the British army, of which the 49th was a unit, was aboard the transports in the Zuyder Zee, off the coast of Holland, and early one morning, under the command of Sir Ralph Abercrombie, with blare of trumpets and standards flying, they effected a landing under the guns of the ships of the line, of which, with frigates and sloops, there were well-nigh sixty. Brock had often listened to the roar of shot and shell in target practice and sham fight, but of a cannonade of artillery, where every shrieking cannon-ball was probably a winged messenger of death, this was his first experience. He now learned that in the music of the empty shell of experiment and the wicked screech of the missiles of war there was an unpleasant difference. He did not wince, but sternly drew himself together, thought of home, begged God's mercy, and awaited the command to advance with an impatience that was physical pain.

By four in the afternoon the Hilder Peninsula and its batteries had been taken, but with a loss to the British of a thousand men. Brock could scarcely believe that the enemy had retreated. This, however, was merely a taste of war. The second division having arrived, the whole force of nearly 20,000 men, under the Duke of York, started to make history. In the last days of a stormy

Egmont-op-Zee and Copenhagen

September 16,000 Russian allies reached the scene. The fourth brigade, which included the 49th, was under the command of General Moore—Sir John Moore, of Corunna fame. For several weeks the waiting troops were encamped in the sand-hills without canvas and exposed to biting storms. The capture of the city of Horn without resistance hardly prepared our hero and his men for the stout opposition at the battle of Egmont-op-Zee that followed.

Brock's brother, Savery, a paymaster to the brigade, though by virtue of his calling exempt from field service, insisted on joining the fighting line, acting as aide to Sir Ralph Abercrombie.

Every record, every line written or in print concerning Brock, from first to last, all prove that the keynote of his success, the ruling impulse of his life, was promptness and action. So, at Egmont, no sooner did the bugle sound the advance than he was off with his men like a sprinter at the crack of the pistol. Others might follow; he would lead. They were part of the advance guard of a column of 10,000 men. The enemy was in front in superior numbers, but their weakness lay in underrating the courage of the British. They had been taught to consider English soldiers the most undisciplined rabble in the world!

This was a factor unknown and unheeded by Brock. All that he knew was that an obstacle barred the way.

.   .   .   .

" Steady, the 49th!"

.   .   .   .

The loud, clear notes of the leader rang above rasping of scabbards and suggestive clank of steel. The men straightened. A suppressed exclamation ran along the line

29

The Story of Isaac Brock

and died to a whisper. Whispers faded into silence. A fraction of a second, perhaps, and then, high above the stillness, when British and French alike were silently appealing to the God of battles, over steaming dyke and yellow sanddunes rose once more in trumpet tones the well-known voice, " Charge, men, and use your bayonets with resolution !" No rules were followed as to the order of going— the ground, to use Brock's words, was too rough, " like a sea in a heavy storm "—but the dogs of war were let loose. The quarry was at bay. Another instant and the air was split with yells, the clash of naked steel and screams of agony. Then cheer upon cheer, as the British swept irresistibly on, and the enemy, declining to face the glittering bayonets and unable to resist the impact of the English, wavered, broke and retreated.

The shedding of men's blood by man is never an edifying spectacle. The motive that prompts the attack or repels it, the blind obedience that entails the sacrifice, the retribution that follows, are more or less understandable. What of the compensation? There may be times when a pure principle is at stake and must be upheld despite all hazards, but there are times when there is no principle at stake whatever. These considerations, however, have no place in the soldier's manual. They are questions for the court, not the camp, and cannot be argued on the battlefield. The soldier is not invited to reason why, though many an unanswerable question by a dying hero has been whispered in the trenches.

There was much carnage at Egmont-op-Zee, and many a 49th grenadier " lost the number of his mess." Isaac directly after the fight wrote to his brothers that " Noth-

Egmont-op-Zee and Copenhagen

ing could exceed the gallantry of his men in the charge."
To his own wound he referred in his usual breezy and
impersonal way. "I got knocked down," he said, "soon
after the enemy began to retreat, but never quitted the
field, and returned to my duty in less than half an hour."

We must appeal to his brother Savery for the actual
facts. "Isaac was wounded," said Savery, in reply to
a request for particulars, "and his life was in all probability preserved by the stout cotton handkerchief which,
as the air was very cold, he wore over a thick black silk
cravat, both of which were perforated by a bullet, and
which prevented it entering his neck. The violence of
the blow, however, was so great as to stun and dismount
him, and his holsters were also shot through."

That the action had been a hot one can be best judged
by the official returns. Out of 391 rank and file of the
49th in the field, there were 110 casualties—30 killed,
50 wounded and 30 missing. Savery Brock shared the
honours with his brother. Oblivious to a hurricane of
bullets, he rode from sand-hill to sand-hill, encouraging
the men until his truancy was noticed and he was halted
by Isaac. "By the Lord Harry, Master Savery," shouted
the colonel, loud as he could pitch his powerful voice, as
the big paymaster strode by, his horse having been shot
under him, "did I not order you, unless you remained
with the General, to stay with your iron chest? Go back,
sir, immediately." To which Savery answered, playfully,
"Mind your regiment, Master Isaac. You surely would
not have me quit the field now." Of this intrepid brother
Isaac wrote, "Nothing could surpass Savery's activity and
gallantry." Another of the wounded at Egmont was Lord

The Story of Isaac Brock

Aylmer, afterwards Governor-General of British North America. The loss of the enemy was estimated at 4,000. Two weeks later the British troops—while suffering intensely from severe weather—met with a reverse in the field, to which, through a misunderstanding of orders, their Russian allies contributed. The Duke of York was ordered to evacuate the country. The campaign had resulted in much experience and high honour for Brock. Quick to perceive and learn, his powers of observation on the field had enriched his mind with lessons in the tactics of war never to be forgotten.

In the ranks of the 49th was a young Irishman of superior talents. Brock was not slow to discover his abilities, and " with a discrimination that honoured both," he later appointed this combative private sergeant-major. Still later he procured him an ensigncy in the 49th, finally appointing him adjutant, promotion that the ability and gallantry of James FitzGibbon, a Canadian veteran of 1812, and the "hero of Beaver Dams" (Adjutant-General of Canada, 1837, and Military Knight of Windsor, 1851), amply justified.

If Brock was quick to appreciate merit, he was no less so in detecting defects. The Russian soldiers came in for scathing criticism. The type at Egmont impressed him most unfavourably. The clumsy Russian foot-soldier was his special aversion. The accuracy of his criticism has been confirmed by military writers, but this book is not for the purpose of weighing the quality of Russian valour in Holland. Six thousand of these Russian allies, the lateness of the season preventing their return home, were later quartered for six months in Guernsey.

COLONEL JAMES FITZGIBBON.

(From photograph by Gerald FitzGibbon.)

Egmont-op-Zee and Copenhagen

While our hero was a severe military critic, he was never an unjust one, neither did he spare his own men. Though not a martinet, which was foreign to every fibre of his nature, he was a stickler for rigid discipline. When the expedition was recalled, he was first quartered in Norwich, and then at the old familiar barracks of St. Helier, in Jersey. On his return to the latter place, in 1800, after leave of absence, he found that the junior lieutenant-colonel of the 49th—Colonel Sheaffe—had incurred the reasonable dislike of the men. The regiment was drawn up on the sands for morning parade, standing at ease. In company with this unpopular officer Brock appeared upon the scene. He was greeted with three hearty cheers. The personal honour, however, was lost sight of in the act of disobedience. Rebuking the men severely for " their most unmilitary conduct," they were marched to quarters and confined to barracks for a week. He would not, he explained, allow public exaltation of himself at the expense of another.

The next year found our hero in the Baltic Sea, aboard the *Ganges,* detailed for active duty as second in command of the land forces that under Lord Nelson were ordered to the attack on Copenhagen. It was intended that Brock, with the 49th, should lead in storming the Trekroner (Three Crown) battery, in conjunction with five hundred seamen; but the heroic defence by the Danes rendered the attempt impracticable, and Brock remained on the *Ganges,* an unwilling spectator of bloodshed in which he took no part. Towards the close of the engagement—the heaviest pounding match in history—he was on the *Elephant,* Nelson's flagship, and saw the hero of

The Story of Isaac Brock

Trafalgar write his celebrated letter to the Crown Prince of Denmark.

As at Egmont, the irrepressible conduct of Savery Brock on the *Ganges* gave our hero much concern. Savery, as a former midshipman, was of course a gunner. While training a quarter-deck gun on the Trekroner battery his hat was blown from his head and he was knocked down by the rush of wind from a grapeshot. Seeing this, Brock exclaimed, " Ah, poor Savery! He is indeed dead." But, to use his own words, it was only " the hot air from the projectile that had ' floored ' him." Previous to this he had driven Isaac almost demented by stating his intention of joining the storming party and sharing his brother's danger. " Is it not enough that one brother should be killed or drowned ?" said Isaac. But Savery persisted until, at Isaac's request, the commander of the *Ganges* kept the paymaster quiet by stratagem. " Master Savery," said he, " you simply *must* remain with us. I appoint you captain of the gun. It will amuse you."

The loss of the Danes at Copenhagen was placed at 6,000, including prisoners. The British killed and wounded numbered 943, more than fell at the Battle of the Nile. Part of this loss is charged to a criminal misconception of military etiquette. To a line officer who asked where his men should be stationed, the captain of the battleship replied, that as soldiers were no good with big guns, and as the forts were out of musket range, he should " send them between decks." This, said the infantryman, " would be eternal disgrace." In deference to this brutal conception of military ethics, the men were drawn up on the gangway and, standing at attention, were allowed to be mowed down by Danish grapeshot. The 49th, on its return to England from Copenhagen, thoroughly initiated in the cruel cult of war, was ordered to Colchester.

Isaac Brock, with the bay-leaves of distinction on his brow, and his heart touched but not dismayed at the ferocity of war, had passed the *second* milestone of his life.

The Story of Isaac Brock

CHAPTER V.

BROCK IN CANADA.

ISAAC BROCK received with regret his orders to proceed with the 49th to Canada. Europe was still in the clutches of war. Great opportunities awaited the soldier of fortune in the struggle waging in the Peninsula. The prospect for military advancement in Canada was not encouraging. America was at peace. Canada was but slowly developing. While her exports of lumber and fish attracted the attention of the British merchant, her great resources were unknown except to the fur trader and the few United States speculators whose cupidity kept pace with their knowledge. Though the known sympathy of the United States for France was regarded as a possible excuse for hostility towards England, as yet this sympathy had found no official utterance, hence the outlook from a soldier's standpoint was far from desirable. Brock's life in the West Indies had created a distaste for garrison duty. While a past master in the details of barrack life, his career under arms had created an aversion for the grind of drill and parade.

Life in the high latitudes of Canada would present a clean-cut contrast to tropical Barbadoes, but it was out of harmony with his ambition, and, judging by his spirits, he might have been embarking for penal servitude at Botany Bay rather than for the land which was to bring him lasting fame. Even the attentions of the devoted

Brock in Canada

Dobson, who had just filled his pipe, did not serve to arouse him. Brock's depression was short-lived. His optimism and faith banished gloomy thoughts. The ship had hardly dropped the last headland of the Irish coast when the winds bred in Labrador awoke the Viking strain in him and filled his soul with hope. The swinging seas of this northern ocean revived thoughts of the long-ago exploits of Sebastian Cabot, the discoverer of Newfoundland, and of his own sea-dog ancestors, those rough-riders of the sea who had defied the banks of Sable Island and returned to St. Peter's Port with their rich cargoes of contraband, looking innocent as kittens, while the ship was bursting with fur, fin and feather. So, pipe in mouth, with the frigate close-hauled, watching her bows splintering the sea into a million jewels, he left care behind, and thenceforward his busy brain was forming plans that would soften his exile in that land of chilling promise he was approaching.

He had been told to expect magnificent scenery, but was quite unprepared for the picture that the Gulf of St. Lawrence unfolded. The Straits of Belle Isle, the Magdalen Islands, the brazen bosom of the Bay of Chaleur that had allured Jacques Cartier 265 years before, the might of the noble river and the glorious vista of the citadel and frowning heights of Quebec, where Wolfe and Montcalm fell—the ancient Stadacona framed in the sunset—amazed him. A presage of coming conflict crowded his brain.

.   .   .   .

"Manfully tell me the truth."

.   .   .   .

37

The Story of Isaac Brock

Carr, an educated soldier of the 49th, was hesitating. Desertions had been frequent at Quebec, and discipline *must* be restored. Stepping up, with hand clenched, the officer continued, " Don't lie! Tell the truth like a man. You know I have ever treated you kindly." The confession of intended desertion followed. " Go, then," said Colonel Brock,—" go and tell your deluded comrades everything that has passed here, and also that I will still treat every man of you with kindness, and then you may desert me if you please."

During the three years of his command at Montreal, York, Fort George and Quebec, though mutiny was epidemic in both Europe and America, Brock had lost but one man by desertion. He had won the loyalty of the rank and file. FitzGibbon said of him that " he created by his judicious praise the never-failing interest of the men in the ranks." His accurate knowledge of human nature served him in the graver experiences of life which followed. His stay in Quebec was short. A study of the ancient citadel and its incomplete fortifications occupied his time. In the summer of 1803 he was stationed at York, a hamlet carved out of the backwoods, sustaining a handful of people, but famous as the gathering-place of many wise men. He found that desertions in Upper Canada had become too frequent. The temptations offered by a long line of frontier easy of access, and the desperate discipline in the army, had led to much brutality in the way of punishments.

Such were the conditions in Upper Canada when Brock reached York. Shortly after his arrival six men, influenced by an artificer, stole a military batteau and

Brock in Canada

started across the lake to Niagara. By midnight Brock, with his trusty sergeant-major and the ever-watchful Dobson, in another batteau with twelve men, passed out of the western gap in hot pursuit of the defaulters. Though the night was calm the trip was perilous. Before them stretched a waste of water, but our hero was in his element. He was living over again his daring visits to the Casquets through the furious seas that raced between St. Sampson and the Isle of Herm.

The crew was divided into "watches," six taking an hour's "breather" while the other six rowed, hour and hour about, alternately rowing and resting. When the wind served they hoisted their big square sail, our hero at the tiller. On this occasion there was little wind, and "Master Isaac," for example's sake, and "to keep my biceps and fore-arm in good condition"—as he told the sergeant-major—took his regular spells at the oar. On arriving at Fort George, Colonel Hunter, Governor and Commandant, rebuked him for rashly venturing across the lake in an open boat, "a risk," he said, "never before undertaken."* The expedition, however, was successful, for the deserters were surprised on the American shore and made prisoners.

* Lake Ontario was crossed from Toronto to the wharf at the mouth of the Niagara River in an ordinary double-scull, lap-strake pleasure-skiff, by the writer and another Argonaut—Herbert Bartlett—one unruly morning in the summer of 1872. Though a risky row, and not previously attempted, it was not regarded as a remarkable feat by the performers.

The Story of Isaac Brock

CHAPTER VI.

BRIDLE-ROAD, BATTEAU AND CANOE.

THE means for transit through Canada at this time was most primitive, and not the least of the questions which occupied Brock's thoughts was the important one of transportation. The lack of facilities for moving large bodies of men and supplies, in event of war, was as apparent as was the lack of vessels of force on lake and river.

Between Quebec and Montreal, a distance of sixty leagues, the overland journey was divided into twenty-four stages, requiring four relays of horse-caleches in summer and horse-carioles in winter. The time occupied was three days, and the rate for travellers twenty-five cents a league. This rough road—which entailed numerous ferries in summer at the Ottawa and at Lake St. Francis, except for a break of fifty miles—led by Cornwall and Prescott to Kingston, along which route United Empire Loyalists twenty years before had established themselves.

A few years prior to Brock's arrival, Governor Simcoe, with the men of the Queen's Rangers, had cut a roadway through the dense forest between Prescott and Burlington, at the head of Lake Ontario. From Ancaster, the then western limit of the U. E. Loyalists' settlement, this road traversed the picturesque region that surrounded the Mohawk village on the Grand River, where Joseph Brant, the famous warrior, was encamped with his Six Nation Indians. From this point it penetrated the roll-

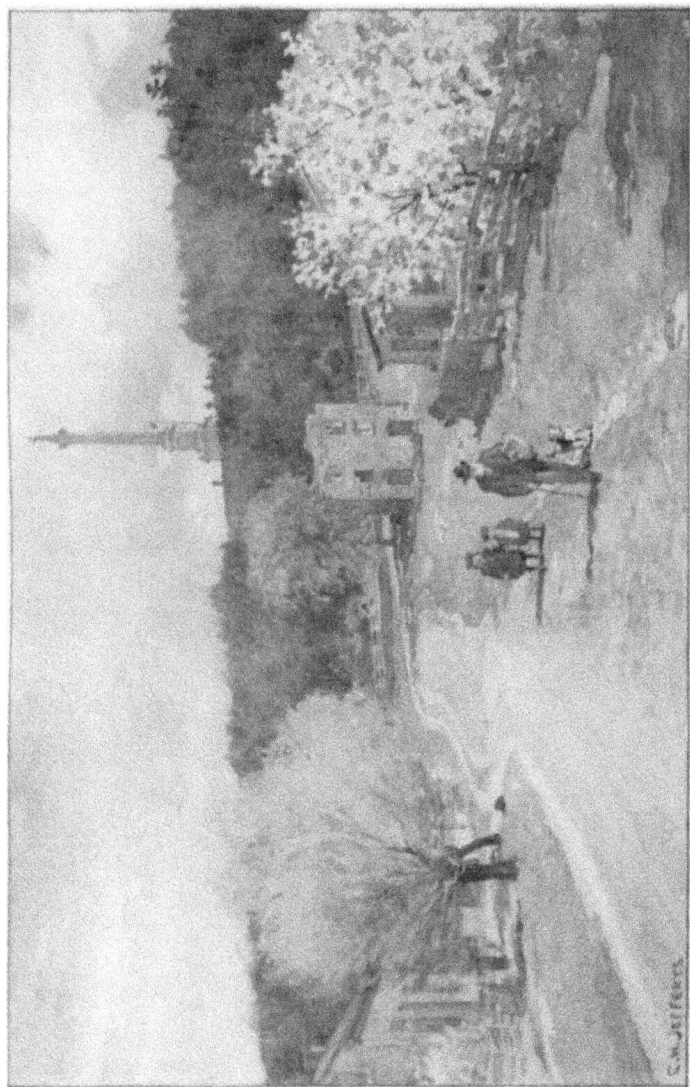

QUEENSTON ROAD ABOUT 1824 (original painting by Charles W. Jefferys, O.S.A.)

Bridle-Road, Batteau and Canoe

ing lands of the western peninsula, to the La Trenche (the Thames River), from whence Lake St. Clair and the Detroit outlet to the great lakes was reached by water. Another military road, also built by Simcoe, followed the old Indian trail through thirty-three miles of forest from York to Lake Simcoe. This shorter route to Lake Superior enabled the North-West Fur Company—established by Frobisher and McTavish, of Montreal, in 1776—to avoid canoeing up the Ottawa and its tortuous tributaries. The batteaux were brought up the St. Lawrence, breaking bulk at certain "carrying places," then under sail up Lake Ontario to York. From here the cargoes were hauled by horses over Yonge's military road to Lake Simcoe, thence by river and stormy Lake Huron to Fort Michilimackinac, Great Turtle Island—the Mackinaw of to-day—at the head of Lake Michigan. By this route fifty dollars was saved on every ton of freight from Ottawa to the middle north. At Mackinaw the goods were reshipped by bark canoe to the still remoter regions in the further West, where Spanish pedlars on the southern tributaries of the lower Mississippi traded with the Akamsea Indians in British goods distributed from Mackinaw.

The records of these trips through a wilderness of forest and stream, with their exhilarating hardships, had a singular fascination for Isaac Brock. It was not long before he had won, with his conquering ways and robust manhood, the allegiance of the big-hearted fur-traders in Montreal. Their wild legends of the great fur country rang in his ears, and his receptive mind was soon stored with the exploits of Radisson and Groseillers, Joliette, Marquette, and other famous pathfinders, with whose

41

The Story of Isaac Brock

exploits a century and a half before, aided by his fluency in French, he became wonderfully familiar.

He found the evolution of the Canadian highway a subject of absorbing interest. From his Caughnawaga guides he learned how the tracks made by lynx and beaver, rabbit and wolverine, wolf and red deer—invariably the safest and firmest ways—were in turn naturally followed by Indian voyageur and fur-trader, until the blazed trail became the bridle-road for the pack-horse of the pioneer. This, as the white settler drifted in, became the winter-road; then, as civilization stifled the call of the wild, there uprose from swamp and muskeg the crude corduroy, expanding by degrees into the half-graded highway, until the turnpike and toll-bar, with its despotic keeper, exacted its tribute from progress. This was the prelude to a still more amazing transformation, for the day soon came, though not in our hero's time, when the drumming of the partridge was silenced by the choo-choo of the locomotive as it shrieked through forest and beaver-meadow on its way to vaster tracks, further and further west, disclosing and leaving in its trail an empire of undreamed-of fertility. Then the redman, disturbed in his solitudes, was confronted with civilization, and had to accept the terms of conquest or seek another sanctuary in the greater wilderness beyond.

The navigation of the lakes and rivers at this time was limited to three types of vessel, the " snow," a three-master with a try-sail abaft the mainmast, the schooner, the batteau and the birch canoe, and, in closely land-locked waters, the horse ferry. The Durham boat, a batteau on a larger scale with false keel, had yet to be introduced. The bark

Bridle-Road, Batteau and Canoe

canoe, which for certain purposes has never been improved upon—not even excepting the cedar-built canoe—varied in size from nine to thirty feet, or, in the language of the voyageur, from one and a half to five fathoms. These canoes had capacity for a crew of from one to thirty men, or a cargo of seventy " pieces " of ninety pounds each, equal to three tons, exclusive of provisions for nine paddlers. In these arks of safety, manned by Indians or *metis* (half-breeds), the fur-trader would leave Lachine, on the St. Lawrence, ascend the Ottawa, descend the French, cross Lake Huron—the Lake Orleans of Nicollet and Hennepin—and find no rest from drench or riffle until he reached Mackinaw, or more distant Fort Dearborn (now Chicago), on the Skunk River, at the head of Lake Michigan, 1,450 miles by water from Quebec.

The batteaux—great, open, flat-bottomed boats, forty feet long and eight feet beam, pointed at stem and stern—were not unlike the York boats used in Lord Wolseley's Red River expedition in 1870, and would carry five tons of cargo. Rigged with a movable mast stepped almost amidships, and a big lug-sail, these greyhounds of the lakes were, for passengers in our hero's time, often the only means of water transport between Quebec and Little York. As important factors in the transport of soldiers and munitions in the war of 1812, they deserve description.

While sailing well when before the wind, they yet, with their defective rig and keelless bottoms, carrying no weather helm, made little headway with the wind close abeam. On one occasion Isaac Brock left Lachine with a brigade of five batteaux, so that all hands could unite in making the portages. At the Cascades, the Milles Roches

The Story of Isaac Brock

and the Cedars, three-quarters of the cargo had to be portaged by the packmen. At times these lightened boats were poled or tracked through the broken water, towed by the men, from such foothold as the rocky banks afforded, by means of a long lariat tied to the boat's bow, with loops over each trackman's shoulder, one man steering with a long sweep. When this treadmill work was impossible, owing to too steep banks, and where no batteau locks existed, the crew hauled the boats across the portage on a skidway of small rolling logs, and, so journeying, Prescott was reached. Here, the wind being favourable, lug-sails were hoisted and Brock's strange fleet started for Kingston, reaching it after twelve days' toil from Lachine, then coasting further along Lake Ontario to Little York (Toronto). When wind failed, the long oars were used, the men rising from the thwarts to pull, standing. Thus, alternately sitting and rising, pulling in unison, the light-hearted voyageurs would break into one of their wild French chants, quaint with catching refrain, in which our hero soon learned to join.

At Prescott Brock sometimes took the Government schooner, paying two guineas for a trip, which might last a week, or caught one of the small " two-stickers " that carried freight between Kingston and Queenston. If much pressed for time, the batteau would be exchanged for a caleche—the stage-coach was as yet only a dream—and he would resign himself to a rude jolting over the colonization road through the forest that flanked the rugged northern shore of Lake Ontario.

These trips were a never-failing source of surprise and profit. The skill of the canoemen, the strength and endur-

Bridle-Road, Batteau and Canoe

ance of the packmen, excited his admiration. What wonderful raw material! Given drill and discipline, what might not be achieved on the frontier with such craftsmen! The muscles, all whipcord, of these rugged Canadians, part *coureur de bois,* part scout, amazed him. One thing was not so evident as he could have wished. Their love seemed to be more for race and language, home and wilderness, than for King and country. Perhaps, as he said, if the safety of their homes were threatened, they would develop patriotism of the highest type.

But, after all, as to kings, "Who," they naively asked him, "was their king? Surely they must be under two flags and two kings. Napoleon or George? *Que voulez vous?*"

As their hearts seemed to be as stout as their limbs, they would, he reflected, be unconquerable, these careless children of waste places. While Brock thus communed, he watched. There was little to choose between them—Narcisse, Baptiste, Louis, Jacques, Pierre—all strong as buffalo, all agile as catamounts.

They would lift the "pieces" from the dripping canoe and land them on the slippery rock. A minute later and Narcisse perhaps would appear, a bit bent, to keep balanced a bag of flour, a chest of tea, a caddy of tobacco and sundry packages of sugar or shot that made up the load resting on his shoulders where body and nape of neck joined. This load was supported and held together by a broad moose-hide band—a tump-line—strapped across his forehead, his upraised hands grasping the narrowing moosehide stretched on either side of his lowered head, between ear and shoulder. Brock would watch these packmen as,

The Story of Isaac Brock

thus handicapped with a load weighing from two to five hundred pounds, they set out across the rough portage, singing, and at a dog trot, following each other in quick succession. There was rivalry, of course, duly encouraged by Brock with a promise of tobacco to the first man in, but it was all good-natured competition, the last man chanting his laughing canzonet as loudly as the first.

Our hero, with his grand physique and cleverness, was not long in mastering the tricks of the carriers. He soon learned to build up a load and adjust a tump-line, after which practice made the carrying of a pack almost twice his own weight a not extraordinary performance.

These trips afforded Brock an opportunity to study Indian character. He learned much from the packman and voyageur that was destined to be of great value to him in his career on the western frontier, among the outposts of civilization.

Little escaped his notice. His faculties were sharpened by contact with these children of the wilds, whose only class-room was the forest, their only teacher, nature. As the crushed blade or broken twig were of deepest import to the Indian scout, so no incident of his life was now too trivial for Brock to dismiss as of no importance.

Mutiny and Desertion

CHAPTER VII.

MUTINY AND DESERTION.

Brock could hardly reconcile the degree of punishment inflicted upon the soldiers, the poorly paid defenders of the Empire, with their casual offences. While he rebelled against the brutalities of some officers, he was powerless to prevent them. The sentencing powers conferred by court-martial were at that time beyond belief. A captain and two subalterns could order 999 lashes with a " cat " steeped in brine. It is on record that on one occasion a soldier was sentenced to 1,500 lashes for " marauding." And there were other modes of torture. This was close upon the heels of a period when even the slightest breaches of the civil law were punished out of all proportion to the offence. While insisting on the strictest discipline, Brock always tempered justice with mercy. Few men better realized the value of a pleasant word or had in such degree the rare tact that permitted familiarity without killing respect.

A terrible incident occurred in the summer of 1803 which tested all Brock's fortitude and conception of duty. A conspiracy to mutiny was discovered at Fort George on the Niagara River. The methods of the commanding officer had exasperated the men until they planned mutiny on a large scale. This included the murder of Colonel Sheaffe and the incarceration of the other officers. A threatening remark by a soldier of the 49th was overheard. He was arrested and put in irons. A confession by another

The Story of Isaac Brock

soldier implicated a well-known sergeant, and a message was sent to York begging Brock's immediate presence.

Our hero landed from the schooner alone. It was dinner hour. The barrack-square, as Brock crossed it to the guard-house, was deserted. In charge of the guard he found two of the suspected ringleaders. The guard presented arms. "Sergeant," said the colonel of towering frame and commanding aspect, "come here. Lay down your pike." The order was promptly complied with. " Take off your sword and sash and lay them down also." This was done. " Corporal O'Brien," said the colonel, addressing the sergeant's brother-conspirator, "bring a pair of handcuffs, put them on this sergeant, lock him up in a cell, and bring me the key." This, too, was done. " Now, corporal, you come here; lay down your arms, take off your accoutrements, and lay them down also." He was obeyed. Turning to the right man of the guard, " Come here, you grenadier. Bring a pair of handcuffs and put them on this corporal, lock him up in another cell, and bring me the key." When this was done, turning to the astounded drummer, our hero said, " Drummer, beat to arms."

The garrison was aroused. First to rush out was Lieutenant Williams, sword in hand. " Williams!" said the Colonel, " go instantly and secure Rock "—a former sergeant, recently reduced. " If he hesitates to obey, even for one second, cut him down." Up the stairs flew Williams, calling to Rock to come down. " Yes, sir," answered Rock, " when I take my arms." " You must come without them," said Williams. " Oh, I must have my arms, sir," and as Rock stretched out his hand to seize his musket in the arm-rack, Williams shouted, " If you lay

Mutiny and Desertion

one finger on your musket I will cut you down," at the same time drawing his sabre. "Now, go down before me." Rock obeyed, was placed in irons, and within half an hour Clark, O'Brien, and nine other mutineers were embarked for York on the schooner.

What a picture rises before us. The mid-day sun, the glittering barrack-square, the scarlet and white tunics and polished side-arms of the frightened soldiers, with Brock, the embodiment of power and stern justice, towering above the shrinking culprits. Expiation of the offence had yet to follow. The appetite of the law had to be appeased. The trial took place at Quebec. Four mutineers and three deserters were condemned to death, and in the presence of the entire garrison were executed. The details of this are best unwritten. Through a shocking blunder, the firing party discharged their carbines when fifty yards distant, instead of advancing to within eight yards of the victims. The harrowing scene rent Brock's heart. That the men who had fought so bravely under him at Egmont and laughed at the carnage at Copenhagen should end their lives in this manner was inexpressibly sad. After reading the account of the execution of their comrades to the men on parade at Fort George, Brock added, " Since I have had the honour to wear the British uniform I have never felt grief like this." The prisoners publicly declared that had they continued under our hero's command they would have escaped their doom, " being the victims of unruly passions inflamed by vexatious authority."

When Brock assumed command every possible privilege was extended to the troops at Fort George. For every request, however trivial, he knew there was some reason. His mind was big enough to trade in trifles.

49

The Story of Isaac Brock

In view of these desertions, the prospect of hostilities between Canada and the United States became a momentous one. By close study of events in France and America and intercourse with prominent United States citizens, Brock detected the signs that precede trouble.

But the grave question of desertion and the war-cloud on the horizon could not occupy our hero's attention to the exclusion of other demands upon his time. Canada's growing importance was attracting many travellers from over-seas. Notable among these was Thomas Moore, the brilliant Irish poet, who was our hero's guest at Fort George for two weeks in the summer of 1803. Every attraction that the peninsula presented was taxed for his entertainment. Of these diversions the one which probably left the most lasting impression on the versatile son of Erin was a gathering of the Tuscarora warriors, under Chief Brant, at the Indian encampment on the Grand River.

" Here," wrote Moore, in one of his celebrated epistles, " the Mohawks received us in all their ancient costumes. The young men ran races for our amusement, and gave an exhibition game of ball, while the old men and the women sat in groups under the surrounding forest trees. The scene altogether was as beautiful as it was new to me. To Colonel Brock, in command of the fort, I am particularly indebted for his many kindnesses during the fortnight I remained with him."

It was while Moore was paddling down the St. Lawrence with his Caughnawaga voyageurs, after leaving Niagara— where he saw the fountains of the great deep broken up— that he composed his celebrated boat-song:

Mutiny and Desertion

" Faintly as tolls the evening chime,
Our voices keep tune and our oars keep time.
Soon as the woods on shore look dim,
We'll sing at St. Ann's our parting hymn.
Row, brothers, row ! the stream runs fast,
The rapids are near, and the daylight's past !"

In the fall of 1805 our hero was gazetted full colonel,
and returned to England on leave. While he had lost
none of the buoyancy of his youth, he was daily realizing
the fullness of his responsibilities.

For the better defence of Canada, he submitted to the
Duke of York, the Commander-in-Chief, a suggestion
for the forming of a veteran battalion. He quoted the
case of the U. E. Loyalists, who after the Revolutionary
war, had been granted small tracts in Upper Canada; con-
trasting their perfect conduct with the practices of some
of the settlers ten years later, whose loyalty, from his own
observation, would not stand the test. Our hero, who was
warmly thanked by the Duke for his zeal, was now
regarded as a person to be reckoned with. His abilities
and charm of manner had won him a reputation at the
Horse Guards.

He returned to Guernsey to receive the congratulations
of those brothers " who loved him so dearly," but had not
time to tell the graphic story of his sojourn in Canada or
revisit the haunts of his boyhood, for news arrived from
the United States of so warlike a character that he
returned before his leave expired. He overtook at Cork
the *Lady Saumarez,* a well-manned Guernsey privateer,
armed with letters of marque, and bound for Quebec.
Leaving London on the 26th of June, 1806, he set sail
for Canada, never to return to those to whom he had so
endeared himself by his splendid qualities.

51

The Story of Isaac Brock

CHAPTER VIII.

FRANCE, THE UNITED STATES AND CANADA.

SHORTLY after his return to Quebec, Isaac Brock succeeded to the command of the troops in both Upper and Lower Canada, with the pay and allowance of a brigadier.

Though no overt act had been committed against Canada by the United States, relations were strained, and he found much to occupy his time. His humanity stirred, he set about erecting hospitals, reorganized the commissariat department, and engaged in an unpleasant dispute with President Dunn, the civil administrator of Lower Canada, regarding the fortifications of the Citadel. To-day deep in plans for mobilizing the militia and the formation of a Scotch volunteer corps of Glengarry settlers; to-morrow devising the best way of utilizing an Indian force in the event of war. In June, 1807, the affair between the British gunboat *Leopard* and the American frigate *Chesapeake* occurred. The former boarded the latter in search of deserters, and on being challenged, gave the *Chesapeake* a broadside. While the *Leopard* was clearly in the wrong, the United States Government rejected every offer of reparation made by Britain. Then came retaliation. French vessels—though France was at war with Britain —were actually allowed by the United States, a neutral power, full freedom of its harbours. The ships of Britain, a power at peace with the United States of America, were refused the same privilege.

For a proper understanding of the position we must

RUINS OF POWDER MAGAZINE, FORT GEORGE.
(From photograph in possession of Miss Carnochan.)

France, the United States and Canada

unroll a page of history. Napoleon, though he crushed the Prussians at Jena, could not efface the memory of his own humiliation at Trafalgar. His ears tingled. He was waiting to deliver a blow that would equalize the destruction of his fleet by Nelson. Though Britain remained mistress of the seas, surely, thought the "little corporal," a way could be found to humble her. If her sources of food supply, for instance, could be cut off, "the wings of her war-ships would be clipped."

To this end Napoleon issued an arrogant proclamation, which was of far-reaching effect. It authorized the destruction of all British goods and all colonial produce shipped to any European port by a British vessel. It allowed the seizure by France of all ships, of whatever nation, which had even *called* at a British port. To this the United States raised no objection, though it was in violation of the world's law in respect to nations which were at peace with each other. The United States' President evidently believed that British resentment at Napoleon's decree would sooner or later provide the United States with an excuse for a disagreement with Britain. He was not mistaken. Britain at once announced that she in her turn would prohibit the ships of other nations visiting French ports until they had first called at a British port. But two wrongs do not make a right. England also, being short of seamen by desertion, insisted that she had the right to search for British seamen on American vessels.

This was a questionable proceeding, and not always carried out in the most amiable manner, as the *Chesapeake* incident proves, and occasionally led to seizing American seamen, native-born citizens of the United States, in mistake for British-born deserters.

The Story of Isaac Brock

Meanwhile Brock found " the military and the people of Quebec divided by opposing elements of dissatisfaction." His call for one thousand men for two months to complete the defences of the Citadel was met by the Provincial Government with what was practically a refusal. He persisted in his purpose, and despite drawbacks which would have deterred a less dominant nature, he erected a battery, mounting eight thirty-six pound guns, raised upon a cavalier bastion, in the centre of the Citadel, so as to command the opposite heights of Point Levis.

Alive to the probability of invasion, and to the defenceless state of the Canadian frontier and the extreme apathy of the Quebec Government, Colonel Brock warned the War Office. He stated that, as the means at his disposal were quite inadequate to oppose an enemy in the field, with a provincial frontier of 500 miles, he would perforce confine himself to the defence of the city of Quebec. The Lower Canadians, willing to undergo training, had formed themselves into corps of cavalry, artillery and infantry, at no expense to the Government, but the Government gave them no encouragement.

This was the state of affairs in Quebec when Lieutenant-General Sir James Craig arrived to take office as Governor-General of the British Provinces in North America as well as Commander of the Forces. Brock soon became the *confidant* of the new administrator, who was not slow to observe the exceptional capacity of our hero. The day came all too quickly for the Governor when occasion arose for the presence of a strong man to take command in Montreal, and with great reluctance he had to call upon Isaac Brock to assume the office.

54

Fur-Traders and Habitants

CHAPTER IX.

FUR-TRADERS AND HABITANTS.

MONTREAL—the Mount Royal of Jacques Cartier—was then in the heyday of its pioneer glory. It was the seat of government of the North-West Company, which exercised feudal sway over an empire of wilderness, lake and prairie, and whose title to monopoly was challenged only by the powerful Hudson's Bay Company. Since 1670 this older syndicate of adventurers had held the destinies of the great lone land in the farther North-West, its fruitful plains and pathless forests, in the hollow of its hand. Later, when the two companies amalgamated, their joint operations extended from Alaska to Rupert's Land, from Oregon to the Sandwich Islands, from Vancouver to Labrador, an empire embracing an area of 4,500,000 square miles.

At Montreal Brock lived with these merchant princes on terms of close intimacy. He was sensible enough, as a man of the world, to enjoy the creature comforts of life. The blazing log-fire, with its glow and crackle, in contrast to the blizzard that raged outside; the dim-lighted splendour of spacious dining-hall, with hewn rafters and savage trophies of the explorers; the polished oak floor and carved ceiling, hung with rare fur and gaudy feathers, appealed to him.

The rubber of whist over, came the fragrant *perfecto*

The Story of Isaac Brock

—these traders ransacked the world for their tobacco—and Brock, under the influence of the soothing weed, would charm these wild vagrants into unlocking some of the strange secrets of the wilderness. From these usually silent but sometimes garrulous merchants he acquired during the long winter nights a fund of facts that greatly influenced his future actions.

Being superseded at Montreal by General Drummond, he did not relish a return to Quebec. Separation from the 49th meant actual pain, but, as he said, "Soldiers must accustom themselves to frequent movements, and as they have no choice, it often happens they are placed in situations little agreeing with their wishes." His regrets were lessened by his promotion to the rank of brigadier-general. But he prayed for active service, still trying to secure a staff appointment in Portugal, and awaited the result of his brother Savery's efforts, hoping he might yet be ordered to join "the best disciplined army that ever left England."

"Your Excellency," he said to the Governor-General, "I *must* see active service, or had much better quit the army, for I can look for no advantage if I remain buried in inaction in this remote corner of the earth, without the least mention ever likely being made of me."

Unsuspected by our hero, fate in his case was only "marking time."

Day after day Brock saw British ships weigh anchor at Quebec with Canadian timber for the building of English vessels of war. The importance of these Canadian provinces to Great Britain awoke in him dreams of a federation of all the colonies. Cargoes of timber,

Fur-Traders and Habitants

that would require more than 400 vessels to transport, were then lying on the beaches of the St. Lawrence. "Bonaparte," he wrote, "coveted these vast colonial areas, and desired to repossess them."

Brock's mind was busy trying to solve these problems. "A small French force of 5,000 men," he told the Governor, "could most assuredly conquer the Province of Quebec. In the event of French invasion, would the volatile Lower Canadian people, in spite of all their privileges, remain loyal?" A certain class of *habitant* argued that Napoleon, who was sure to conquer Europe, would of course seize the Canadas, encouraged by the United States. "Would Englishmen," asked Brock, "if positions were reversed, be any more impatient to escape from possible British rule than were French Canadians from the possible rule of France?"

"Blood, my good FitzGibbon," he declared to his *protégé*, "is thicker than water. You cannot expect to get men to change their nature, or the traditions of their race, through an act of parliament at twenty-four hours' notice. Old thoughts and habits die hard."

Though Brock's perceptive faculties were well developed, his forecasts, built upon the evidences of opposition among certain Lower Canadians, happily proved only in part correct. Later, when his plan of campaign was menaced by still greater disaffection in Upper Canada, he found he had not reckoned on the influence of his own example, which, added to his power of purpose, "disconcerted the disloyal." In proof of this fact Detroit and Queenston Heights were splendid examples.

It was this spirit of unrest among the people of Quebec

The Story of Isaac Brock

that moved Sir James Craig to keep Brock within easy reach until the growing discord in Upper Canada called for the presence of a man of tact and resolution, one to whom all things seemed possible—and Brock knew no such word as " impossible." On one occasion the " faithful sergeant-major " had ventured to declare that a certain order was " impossible." " ' Impossible !' " repeated Brock, " nothing should be ' impossible ' to a soldier. The word ' impossible ' must not be found in a soldier's vocabulary."

The Massacre at Mackinaw

CHAPTER X.

THE MASSACRE AT MACKINAW.

IT was while stationed in Montreal that our hero met
Alexander Henry, ex-fur-trader and adventurer and
coureur de bois—then a merchant and King's auctioneer
—a notable personage and leader in many a wild exploit
in the far West, an old though virile man after Isaac's
own heart.

From Henry he learned much of the Indian wars in
the West, and the strategic value of various points on the
frontier, possession of which in the event of war he foresaw would be worth a king's ransom. Not least were
details respecting Michilimackinac, the Mackinaw already
referred to. Nearly half a century before, Henry, a
native of New Jersey, of English parents—his ambition
fired by tales of the fabulous fortunes to be made in the
fur trade—obtained from the commandant at Montreal
a permit to proceed west as a trader. He outfitted at
Albany, and the following summer set out for Mackinaw.

Meanwhile the Indian allies, under control of the great
Pontiac, were fighting immigration and civilization.
Between Fort Pitt—Pittsburgh—and the Fox River, in
Wisconsin, the home of the Sacs and Foxes, they had
captured nine out of thirteen military posts, and were
secretly planning the downfall of Fort Mackinaw. This
was regarded as an impregnable post and vulnerable only
through strategy—in Indian parlance another name for

The Story of Isaac Brock

duplicity. Fort Mackinaw, as Brock well knew, was the most important trading *entrepôt* west of Montreal. It served a territory extending from the Missouri in the west to the far Kissaskatchewan in the north.

On Henry's arrival his friendship was sought by an Indian chief, Wawatam. Between these two men a remarkable attachment developed. They became brothers by mutual adoption. At this time the fort was garrisoned by ninety British regulars. One day, outside the walls on the surrounding plateau, several hundred savages were encamped, ostensibly for purposes of trade, some of them killing time by playing the Indian game of ball—the *baggatiway* of the red-man, *la jeu de la crosse* of the voyageur. Henry, acting upon a veiled warning by Wawatam, suggested to the officer in command extra precaution.

"I told him," said he, while Brock drank in every word, "that Indian treachery was proverbial." Now this recital was of the deepest interest to our hero, for Mackinaw, then in the possession of the United States, held the key to the Michigan frontier and control of the upper lakes. While the huge log fire that roared in the chimney cast light and shadow on polished wall and the oak beams of the big dining-hall, Brock puffed away at his huge *partiga,* weighing every word that fell from the bearded lips of the trader.

"Major Errington," continued Henry, "while thanking me, laughed at my forebodings. Then Wawatam urged me, as his adopted brother, to depart for Sault Ste. Marie. But I delayed and once more sought Errington, who still ridiculed my fears. While I was yet expostulat-

The Massacre at Mackinaw

ing with him we heard the louder shouts of the Indians. They had rushed through the fort gateway into the enclosure within the palisades in pursuit of a lost ball. This was but a ruse to gain admittance, for in a moment the laughter and shouts changed to wild yells and war-whoops. The guard was overpowered in a flash, and in the attack that followed almost the entire garrison was tomahawked and scalped."

"Ah!" said Brock, "so British lethargy and self-complaisance succumbed to Indian duplicity."

Then his thoughts turned to Niagara. He saw the open portals of Fort George, and Tuscarora youths playing the Indian game of ball in the meadows of the Mohawk village.

"Those who escaped massacre at Mackinaw," said Henry, refilling his stone pipe and resuming his story, "were preserved for a worse fate. Pontiac's allies—and you, Colonel, know something of these matters from the tales told you by the officers of the North-West Company—entered on a carnival of blood. From a garret, where a Pawnee Indian woman had secreted me, I saw the captured soldiers tomahawked and scalped, and some butchered like so many cattle, just as required for the cannibal feast that followed."

"Tortured?" interrogated Brock.

"Tortured!" repeated Henry. "Why, the diabolical devices that those men resorted to to inflict acute physical agony were inconceivable—unutterable, Colonel." He paused. . . . "After all, no worse, perhaps, than the tortures that have been inflicted by civilized fanatics in Europe."

There was silence for a moment. Both men were buried

61

The Story of Isaac Brock

deep in thought, the one living in the past, the other striving to forecast the future.

"Through the intercession of Wennway, another friendly Indian," continued Henry, "my life was spared. Preparations were made for my secret departure. As I shoved my canoe into the water, *en voyage* for Wagoshene, the prayers of Wawatam rang in my ears as, standing on the yellow beach with outstretched arms, he invoked the *Gitche Manitou,* the Great Spirit, to conduct me in safety to the wigwams of my people."

"Surely, Master Henry," commented Isaac Brock, "with all the latent qualities for good that seem to underlie the outward ferocity of some redmen, firmness and kindness are alone needed to convert them into faithful friends."

"An Indian, or Indians collectively," said Henry, pausing before he answered,—"I speak from personal experience only—are faithful so long as you keep absolute good faith with them. In this particular they are no different from white people; but never deceive them, even in trifles, and never subject them to ridicule. Then, if you treat them with consideration, you can reasonably depend upon their individual loyalty. They expect a lot of attention. Yes! an Indian is naturally grateful, probably far more so than the ordinary white man, and seldom forgets a kindness. Should you come into closer contact with the redman, Colonel, as I have a presentiment you will before long, never forget that an Indian, by right of his mode of life, is deeply suspicious and painfully sensitive. He has a keen sense of humour, however, and is quick to discern and laugh at the weak points of others,

The Massacre at Mackinaw

which, until you understand his language, you will be slow to suspect. On the other hand, he won't stand being laughed at himself or placed in a foolish position. For that matter, who can? Occasionally you will meet a savage with strangely high principles. Among the redskins there is a proportion of good and bad, as there is in all races, but less crime, under normal conditions, than there is among the whites. So, summing up his vices and virtues, the North American Indian, allowing for heredity and surroundings, differs little from ourselves."

"They are brave," interrupted Brock.

"Oh, yes," said Henry, "splendidly reckless of life. The courage of the fatalist I should say. You see, they are so constantly on the war-path that fighting is a compulsory pastime."

"Still," said Brock, "with what daring they fight for their homes."

"True, Colonel," retorted Henry, "but when it comes to fighting for home, a hummingbird will defend its nest. Their peculiar traits are largely the result of a nomadic life and tribal strife, hence their duplicity. Superstition influences them greatly, as it does all savage races. In one respect they are at least superior to some of our own people—I refer to their treatment of their children. Their lovingkindness is pathetic. Contact with civilization, as you may discover, develops at first all their bad qualities, for they are apt imitators, so when the pagan Indian meets a trader without a conscience—and there are some, you know—why, he is not slow to adopt the bad Christian's methods."

The Story of Isaac Brock

CHAPTER XI.

LITTLE YORK, NIAGARA, AMHERSTBURG.

In common with most great men, Brock found distraction in trifles. For weeks prior to leaving Quebec all kinds of gayety prevailed. A visit from Governor Gore of Upper Canada, and the arrival of the fleet from Guernsey and two frigates from Portsmouth, gave a fillip to society. Races, water-parties and country picnics were the order of the day. Our hero's contribution consisted of a banquet and grand ball. He had his own troubles, however, that even the versatile Dobson could not overcome, and he roundly scolded his brother Irving for not sending him a new cocked hat.*

"That cocked hat," he said, "has not been received; a most distressing circumstance, as from the enormity of my head I find the utmost difficulty in getting a substitute."

His departure for York weighed upon him. In Quebec he had the most "delightful garden imaginable, with abundance of melons and other good things"—these,

---

*Miss Carnochan, as the Curator of the Niagara Historical Society the custodian of many relics of the war of 1812, has in her keeping this identical cocked hat. It arrived "shortly after Brock's death, and was given by his nephew to Mr. George Ball, near whose residence the 49th was stationed. The hat measures twenty-four inches inside, and was used at the funeral obsequies of 1824 and 1853, when many old soldiers requested, and were permitted, to try it on." The usage that the cocked hat then received has not improved its appearance.

BROCK'S COCKED HAT
(Water color sketch, from original photo, by Harry Carter.)

Little York, Niagara, Amherstburg

together with his new bastions and forts, he had to desert. Being somewhat of a philosopher, he said that since fate decreed the best portion of his life was to be wasted in inaction, and as President Jefferson, though he wanted war, was afraid to declare it, he supposed he should have to be pleased with the prospect of moving upwards.

Brock had been but a few weeks at Fort George—a " most lonesome place," as compared with Quebec, Montreal, Kingston, or even Little York, from which latter place he was cut off by forty miles of lake, or more than a hundred miles of dense forest and bridgeless streams— when he decided upon a flying trip to Detroit, where, during the French *régime,* the adventurous Cadillac had landed in 1701. He would inspect the western limit of the frontier now under his care and obtain at first hand a knowledge of the peninsula. " For," as he remarked to Glegg, his aide, " if I can read the signs aright, the two nations are rushing headlong into a military conflict."

Two routes were open to him, one overland, the other land and water. He chose the latter. A vast quantity of freight now reached Queenston from Kingston. Vessels of over fifty tons sailed up the river, bearing merchandise for the North-West Company. Salt pork from Ireland and flour from London, Britain being the real base of supply—the remote North-West looking to Niagara for food and clothing—the return cargoes being furs and grain. To portage these goods around Niagara Falls kept fifty or more farmers' waggons busy every day during the summer. A team of horses or oxen could haul twenty " pieces," of one hundred weight each, for a load. The entire length of the portage from Lake Ontario to

The Story of Isaac Brock

Lake Erie was practically a street, full of all the bustle and activity that a scattered country population of 12,000 conferred upon it. Two churches, twenty stores, a printing house, six taverns and a scholastic academy supplied the varied wants of Niagara's 500 citizens who overfilled its one hundred dwellings.

From Lake Ontario, Newark, as it had been called, presented an inviting appearance. The brick-and-stone court-house and jail and brightly painted Indian council-house and cottages rose in strong contrast against the green forest. On the river bank was Navy Hall, a log retreat for seamen, and on Mississaga (Black Snake) Point a stone lighthouse flashed its red signal of hope to belated mariners. Nearer the lake shore, in isolated dignity across a mile of common, stood Fort George, a dilapidated structure with wooden palisades and bastions. Half-acre lots in the village were given gratis by the Government to anyone who would build, and eight acres outside for inclosures, besides a large " commonty " for the use of the people. A quite pretentious wharf lined the river, and from this, on any summer afternoon, a string of soldiers and idle citizens might be seen—among whom was Dobson—casting hook and troll for bass, trout, pickerel and herring, with which the river swarmed. On one occasion Brock helped to haul up a seine net in which were counted 1,008 whitefish of an average weight of two pounds, 6,000 being netted in one day.

Side-wheel ferries, driven by horse-power, plied between the river's mouth and the Queenston landing. The paddle-wheels of these were open double-spoke affairs, without any circular rim. A stage-coach also ran between Queens-

Little York, Niagara, Amherstburg

ton and Fort Erie, the first in Upper Canada. For one dollar the passenger could travel twenty-five miles.

At Fort Erie, at the head of the Niagara River, Brock embarked in mid-August in a government schooner. He wished to familiarize himself with the upper water-ways. He made the long trip from Quebec to York, and thence to Niagara, Amherstburg, Detroit, Sandwich and return overland to Fort George, within two months—record time. Dobson accompanied his master. Brock was silent as to his impressions, but admitted he was convinced that the water route for a military expedition was the only practical one, and that Mackinaw, held by the United States, was the portal and key to the western frontier in case of invasion. He crossed overland through the "bad woods" and open plains to the Point of Pines, where batteaux and canoes awaited him. From thence he proceeded along the north shore of Lake Erie until abreast of the Miami, a confluent of the Ohio River, on the south shore, then turned northward up the Detroit River, twenty-five miles farther, reaching Amherstburg—called Malden by the Americans—250 miles from Fort Erie. Here, after consulting with Colonel St. George, he inspected the battery at Sandwich, and with little ceremony visited Detroit— the old military post of Pontchartrain—on the opposite side of the river, later notorious as an emporium for "rum, tomahawks and gunpowder." From Amherstburg, a small village with an uncompleted fort and shipyard, he sent messengers to the remote post of St. Joseph, an island, fifty-five miles from Mackinaw, below Sault Ste. Marie, and started homewards overland.

In returning, he skirted the great tributary marshes,

67

The Story of Isaac Brock

alive with water-fowl of every description, whose gabble and flapping wings could be heard at a long distance. He camped in the vast hardwood forests that covered the western point of the peninsula that extends west from Lake Ontario to the river connecting Lake Huron with Lake Erie. He shot big bustards and wild turkeys in the bush, where wolves and deer were as thick as rabbits in a warren, and tramped the uplands, teeming with quail and prairie chicken. Continuing by Delaware and the Government road at Oxford on the Thames, and by the "Long Woods" over the Burford Plains to Brant's Ford, he reached the Grand River, and then by Ancaster and the head of the lake to Burlington, when he followed the Lake Ontario southern shore road to Niagara.

Many of the settlers whom he met were from the Eastern States. These were the original Loyalists or their descendants, patriots to the core. Other more recent arrivals—perhaps two-thirds of the whole—came from Pennsylvania, New York and New Jersey, attracted by the fertility of the soil and freedom from taxation, or to escape militia service. These latter he quickly realized were not the class to rely upon in event of war, but he gave no public sign of distrust. It was from the pick of the first-mentioned stalwarts that Brock formed his loyal Canadian militia, his gallant supporters in the war of 1812, who made a reputation at Detroit and Queenston that will never die.

He was more than ever sensible of the resources of the country. This glimpse of the west enamoured him. To his "beloved brothers"—our hero always thus addressed them—he described it as a "delightful country, far exceed-

Little York, Niagara, Amherstburg

ing anything I have seen on this continent." The extent of the Great Lakes amazed him, as did their fish. From these deep cisterns he had seen the Indian fishermen take whitefish, the *ahtikameg* (deer-of-the-water), twenty pounds in weight; maskinonge—*matchi-kenonje,* the great pike—more than twice that size, and sturgeon that weighed two hundred pounds and over, and in such quantities that he hesitated to tell his experiences on his return.

Henry's stories of five hundred whitefish taken with a scoop net at the rapids of Sault Ste. Marie in two hours were no longer questioned. The size of the red-fleshed land-locked trout (the quail-of-the-water), of pickerel and bass, astounded him. His travels had broadened his views. The chatter of his Iroquois and Algonquin friends was now easier of interpretation. The riddles of the wilderness were more easily read. He now realized how possible it was, in this continent of unsurveyed immensity, to journey for weeks, after leaving the white man's domain hundreds of miles behind, and then reach only the rim of another kingdom of even far greater fertility. He also realized that beyond these laughing lands lay a rugged world of desolation, bounded in turn by the rasping ice-floes of the Arctic.

If Brock's mind had expanded, so had his body. He was, as he expressed it, as "hard as nails." The close of 1811 found "Master Isaac" a grand specimen of manhood. Inclined to be a little portly, he was still athletic. His face, though a trifle stern, had grown more attractive, because of the benevolent look now stamped upon it. He was still fair and florid, with a broad forehead, and eyes though somewhat small, yet full and of a grayish blue,

The Story of Isaac Brock

a charming smile and splendid white teeth. Always the same kindly gentleman and always a soldier. His life at Fort George had been one of great loneliness. He read much and rapidly, and would memorize passages from the books that had left the deepest impression. History, civil and military, especially ancient authors, was his choice, and maps his weakness. Over these, with his devoted aides, he would pore late into the night, until he knew the country almost as well as his friend the Surveyor-General. For variety he feasted upon the robust beauties of Pope's " Homer," ever regretting he never had a master " to guide and encourage him in his tastes."

With Lieutenant-Governor Gore, formerly a soldier in Guernsey, our hero was on intimate terms. When the grind of duty let him, he would travel " the worst road in the country—fit only for an Indian mail-carrier—in order to mix in the society of York." He periodically returned these hospitalities by a grand ball at Niagara —always the event of the season. Brock, while fond of women's society, preferred brain to beauty. Had his old Guernsey friends been present on these occasions they would not have recognized in the soldier, resplendent in a general's uniform, now dancing a mazurka, the handsome stripling who only a few years since had waltzed his way into the hearts of all the women of St. Peter's Port.

The unrest of the Indians at Amherstburg troubled him. He had seen over eight hundred in camp there, receiving rations for a month while waiting presents of blankets, powder and shot from King George. They asked British support if they took the warpath against the Americans— the Long-knives—*Gitchi-mokohmahn,* their sworn enemies.

70

Little York, Niagara, Amherstburg

Tecumseh, a Shawanese chief, had demanded from the United States the restoration of violated rights. This demand had not been complied with. The position was critical. Great tact was required to retain the friendship of the Indians, while not complying with their request.

In Lower Canada there was still discord among the French Canadians. The Governor, Sir James Craig, in a dying condition, relinquished office. In answer to Brock's application for leave, still hoping for a staff appointment in Portugal, the Governor-General implored him to remain.

"I must," he told him, "leave the country in the best state of security I can; your presence is needed here. I am sending you as a mark of my sincere regard my favourite horse, Alfred." This was a high-bred animal, and our hero's charger in the war that followed.

It was not, however, until war was regarded as unavoidable, and not until after he was promoted to be a major-general and appointed President and Administrator of Upper Canada, as successor to Governor Gore, that Isaac Brock became reconciled to life in Canada, and with set purpose assumed the duties of his high calling.

. . . .

Our hero had passed his *third* milestone.

The Story of Isaac Brock

CHAPTER XII.

MAJOR-GENERAL BROCK, GOVERNOR OF UPPER CANADA.

The appointment of Brock—with his exceptional military attainments—to the chief command in Upper Canada, at the point of greatest danger, was a rare piece of good fortune for the colony. Of the American military leaders, Generals Howe, Dearborn and Wadsworth were all examples of a common standard; even Sir George Prevost, the new Governor-General of Canada and Commander-in-Chief, was tuned in a minor key.

Isaac Brock was the man of the hour. His star was in the ascendant. Queen Victoria's father, the Duke of Kent, was anxious to meet the soldier whose despatches had stirred the War Office. The Duke of York was ready to give him a brigade under Wellington, while the Governor of Jamaica, the Duke of Manchester, then touring Canada, begged Brock, whom he looked upon as a " universal provider," to equip him with canoes and guides for a western pilgrimage. If Brock's promotion brought him distinction it also brought him work—Executive Councils, court-martials, reorganization of militia, reconstruction of the ruined forts on the Niagara frontier, the building of gun-boats, the making of roads. Never idle. To-day he was inspecting a camp of the 49th at Three Rivers, near Montreal; next week at Fort Erie. Ever busy, ever buoyant. Whether perusing documents, scouring the muddy roads at Queenston, surveying the boundaries of the dreaded Black Swamp, or visiting the points between

72

Gen. Brock, Governor of Upper Canada

Fort George and Vrooman's battery on his slashing gray charger, he had a smile and cheery word for everyone. As for Dobson, his profound awe at his master's progress was only equalled by his devotion, that increased with the illness that threatened his life; while the faithful sergeant-major, now Captain FitzGibbon, in command of a company of the 49th, was reflecting great credit on his patron. But no matter what the tax on his time, Isaac never neglected the "beloved brothers."

In New York there had been financial failures. Brock predicted a dreadful crash, and had so written to his brother Irving, who with William had a bank in London. He hoped they "had withheld their confidence in public stocks." Providence ruled otherwise. While Isaac in the solitude of his quarters was writing this warning, the banking house in London, whose vessels in the Baltic Sea had been seized by Bonaparte's privateers, closed its doors. The news reached him on his birthday. He learned that a private advance made to him by William for the purchase of his commissions had been entered in the bank's books by mistake. He was a debtor to the extent of £3,000.

Brock rose to the occasion. He proved himself not only a soldier but, best of all, a just man with the highest sense of personal honour. His distress was all for his brothers. He would sell his commission, turn over his income as governor and surrender everything, if by doing so he could save the fortunes of his family. Anything that not only the law but the right might demand. This failure impaired the former good fellowship between William and Irving Brock. Isaac wrote Irving, beseeching him to repair the breach. "Hang the world," said he; "it is not worth a thought. Be generous, and find

The Story of Isaac Brock

silent comfort in being so. Oh, my dear brother, forget the past and let us all unite in soothing the grief of one of the best hearts that heaven ever formed, whose wish was to place us all in affluence. Could tears restore him he would be happy."

But Isaac was not permitted to know that reconciliation followed his prayers. While William and Irving were shaking hands, but before they had even heard of the capture of Detroit, Isaac, unknown to them, was at that moment lying cold in death within the cavalier bastion at Fort George.

Little York was now Brock's headquarters. He built dockyards to shelter His Majesty's navy, which consisted of two small vessels! He planned new Parliament Buildings and an arsenal, prepared township maps showing roads and trails, fords and bridges, all of which latter were in a shocking condition. At York the timber and brushwood was so dense that travel between the garrison and town was actually by water. His mind made up that war with the United States was inevitable, he was confronted with crucial questions demanding instant solution. Chief of these was the defence of the frontier, 1,300 miles in length, which entailed repairs of the boundary forts, the raising of a reliable militia, the increase of the regular troops, the building of more gunboats, and the solving of the Indian problem.

BUTLER'S BARRACKS (OFFICERS' QUARTERS), NIAGARA COMMON.

The War Cloud

CHAPTER XIII.

THE WAR CLOUD.

A PRESIDENT of the United States had breezily declared that the conquest of Canada would be " a mere matter of marching." The final expulsion of England from the American continent he regarded as a matter of course. Cabinet ministers at Washington and rabid politicians looked upon the forcible annexation of Canada as a foregone conclusion.

One Massachusetts general officer, a professional fire-eater, said he " would capture Canada by contract, raise a company of soldiers and take it in six weeks." Henry Clay, another statesman, " verily believed that the militia of Kentucky alone were competent to place Upper Canada at the feet of the Americans." Calhoun, also a " war-hawk," had said that " in four weeks from the time of the declaration of war the whole of Upper and part of Lower Canada would be in possession of the United States." All of this was only the spread-eagle bombast of amateur filibusters, as events proved, but good cause for Brock, who had been appointed janitor of Canada and been given the keys of the country, to ponder deeply.

Canada's entire population was nearly 320,000—about the same as that of Toronto to-day—that of the United States was 8,000,000! To defend her broken frontier Canada had only 1,450 British soldiers and a militia —at that moment—chiefly on paper. If the Indians in

The Story of Isaac Brock

the West were to be impressed with British supremacy—for they were making a stand against 2,000 American soldiers on the banks of the Wabash, in Ohio, where eighteen years before they had been beaten by General Wayne at Miami—then Amherstburg must be greatly strengthened and the Americans deterred from attack. How was Brock to obtain troops, and how were they to be equipped? The stores at Fort York were empty, provisions costly, and no specie to be had. All the frontier posts needed heavier batteries. On Lake Erie the fleet consisted of the *Queen Charlotte* and the small schooner *Hunter*. As to the militia, he had been advised that it would not be prudent to arm more than 4,000 of the 11,000 in all Canada prepared to bear arms.

To Brock's citation of thirty pressing wants Sir George Prevost wrote him, "You must not be led into any measure bearing the character of *offence,* even should war be declared." Prevost had a fluid backbone, while Brock's was of finely tempered steel.

While affairs were in this precarious state His Excellency the Lieutenant-Governor, Major-General Brock, opened the Legislature at York. With what pride the news was received by the good people at St. Peter's Port can be imagined. To think that this great man, gorgeous in a purple Windsor uniform and slender court sword, with gleaming silk hose and hair aglitter with silver powder, was none other than " Master Isaac," whom the humblest Guernsey fisherman claimed as comrade, seemed past belief! To think that this important gentleman, with frilled waistcoat and cuffs of delicate lace—actually the King's Deputy—before whom, as " Your Excellency," Indian and paleface, gentle and simple, bowed low, was

The War Cloud

the small boy who used to play " uprooting the gorse " with the Guernsey fisher-lads—was beyond comprehension. Probably the one least affected by these honours was our hero himself. While it gratified his honest pride, it did not in the least cloud his vision. His speech from the throne proves this.

" It is a glorious contest in which the Empire is engaged," he said, " to secure the independence of Europe, but what can we think of the American Government, which is trying to impede her effort. . . . The ships of England," he continued, " had been refused shelter in United States harbours, while refuge had been extended to the ships of our inveterate enemies." He reminded the colonists that " insulting threats had been offered to the flag and hostile preparations made." He praised the militia, and, while wishing for peace, declared that " Canada must prepare for war, relying on England's support in her hour of peril." He asked the Legislature to assent to three things of vital importance—the suspension of the Habeas Corpus Act, the passage of a law to regulate the privileges of aliens, and an Act providing for rewards to be paid to the captors of deserters.

It was a house divided against itself, and it turned a deaf ear to Brock's appeal. " To the great influence of *American settlers* over the members of the Lower House," he attributed this defeat. A court-martial revealed the fact that one of the best known militia regiments was composed almost entirely of native Americans! The United Empire Loyalists thronged to his banner.

Undaunted by the cheap prudence of Prevost, a hostile Legislature, and the difficulties that beset him, Brock took off his coat, rolled up his sleeves, and all but single-handed

The Story of Isaac Brock

—" off his own bat," as Dobson explained it to an admiring crowd in the barrack-room—wrought like the hero that he was for the salvation of his country. He became a machine, a machine working at high pressure eighteen hours out of twenty-four. He had developed into a very demon for work.

With an empty treasury and no hope of reinforcements —every soldier England could spare was fighting in Spain —he raised flank companies of militia to be attached to the regular regiments. The Glengarry sharpshooters, four hundred strong, were enlisted in three weeks. A new schooner was placed on the stocks. He formed a car-brigade of the young volunteer farmers of York and removed incompetent officers.

Fort George, constructed of earthen ramparts, with honeycombed cedar palisades which a lighted candle could set fire to, with no tower or block-house, and mounting only nine-pound guns, he knew was incapable of resistance. It invited destruction from any battery that might be erected at Youngstown on the American side, while confronting it was Fort Niagara, built of stone, mounting over twenty heavy guns, containing a furnace for heating shot, and formidable with bastions, palisades, pickets and dry ditch. The tension at Niagara was trying. Two officers of the 41st were expelled for killing dull care by dissipation. A Canadian merchant schooner was boarded in mid-lake by an American brig, taken to Sackett's Harbour and stripped. The Americans were pouring rations and munitions of war into Detroit. If Brock's hands were shackled, he knew the art of sitting tight. He made another flying trip to Amherstburg, taking one hundred men of the 41st, in the face of Prevost's standing orders to " exercise the

The War Cloud

strictest economy." Handicapped on every side, doing his best and preparing for the worst, he wrote Prevost that his "situation was critical," but he "hoped to avert dire calamity."

The river bank between Fort George and Queenston for seven miles was patrolled night and day. A watch was placed on Mississaga lighthouse from daylight to dusk, and beacon masts, supporting iron baskets filled with birchbark and pitch, were erected on the heights to announce, in event of hostilities, the call to arms.

At this time one of Brock's most intimate friends—his chosen adviser—was Mr. Justice William Dummer Powell, later Chief Justice of Upper Canada, and former Speaker of the House. At the judge's house and at Tordarroch, the log mansion of General Æneas Shaw—another intimate, and Adjutant-General of Militia—Brock was wont to repair for a few hours' rest from official cares. It was at Tordarroch (Oak Hall), on the outskirts of York, that the great Duke of Kent had been a guest. When at Fort George our hero usually lived with Colonel Murray, of the 100th, and "charming Mrs. Murray," as he was fond of calling her, in their "pretty cottage," and if not there he was a constant visitor at the house of Captain John Powell, a son of the judge and son-in-law of General Shaw, between whose daughter, Sophia Shaw, and Isaac Brock there had developed a deep attachment. Here he whiled away spare moments with whist and cribbage, "diversions," he said, "that sharpened a man's wits." He would shoot wild pigeons and spruce partridges in the adjacent bush, or take long gallops, frequently alone, over the plains beyond the Heights of Queenston, ever on the lookout for new bridle-paths and point-to-point trails.

The Story of Isaac Brock

CHAPTER XIV.

THE UNITED STATES OF AMERICA DECLARES WAR.

IT came at last! On June 18th, 1812, after weeks of preparation, placing an embargo on shipping, putting 100,000 militia on a war footing on the pretence of hostilities among the Indians, calling out the volunteers and raising a special public fund, Congress under President Madison declared war against Great Britain.

This did not end Brock's suspense. Not until five weeks later did he receive official notice from Prevost. Despite opposition from many states, which declared their detestation of an alliance with Bonaparte, after a stormy debate behind closed doors at Washington, Congress voted for war against England, with Canada as the point of attack. The United States placed itself on record as approving of " forcible invasion of a neighbouring peaceful country and its rights, and of taking property on which it had no shadow of claim."

The offensive " right of search " of American ships by British warships for deserters was, of course, given as the excuse for war. The United States Government contended that a nation's flag protected the cargoes of the vessels of that nation. To search for contraband or for deserters on such ships, President Madison declared, was a violation of international law. In direct violation of the United States' own interpretation of this decree, her war-frigate *President* blew the British gunboat *Little Belt,*

The United States of America Declares War

half her own size, almost out of the water because of the refusal of her commander to allow such search.

It is interesting to remember that while the United States contended that Britain had no right to search the ships of other nations, she actually allowed her own officials, in the case of an American sailor who had become a citizen of France and an officer in the French navy, to search the foreign vessel upon which he served and arrest him as a deserter. A more flagrant violation of the principles she professed is difficult to imagine. She insisted that this officer was still a citizen of the United States, for he could not become a citizen of another country without the consent of the government of his native country. So, when it suited her purpose, and in direct defiance of her own proclamation, she did not hesitate to accept England's contention and adopt the "obnoxious doctrine"—thus practising the identical principle against which she had declared war. Truly glaring inconsistency.

While these were the chief of the alleged reasons for war, the whole world knew that the real cause was the jealousy and hatred felt for England by a certain class of United States citizens who "were bound to pick a quarrel with John Bull, excuse or no excuse." That there were many and irritating faults on the part of England cannot be denied. In the light of subsequent events it is not difficult to realize that both governments were in the wrong. The wisdom born of bitter experience and the sincere friendship of the two nations to-day, sensibly founded on mutual respect, happily renders a repetition of such regrettable scenes outside the pale of possibility.

Strange to say, England had revoked the objectionable Order-in-Council authorizing right of search of American

The Story of Isaac Brock

ships for deserters by British men-of-war the very day *before* war was declared by the United States. There was no ocean cable in those days. Had there been, this story might never have been written. The removal, however, of this one reason for *war* was not—when letters duly arrived from England announcing the fact—accepted by the United States as a reason for an immediate declaration of *peace*. This proves that the reasons advanced by the United States for going to war were from first to last not genuine, but mere excuses. Canada was as Naboth's vineyard, and Ahab, in the person of the United States, coveted it. England hesitated to draw the sword on a people "speaking a common tongue, with institutions based upon her own," but she could not always be expected to "turn the other cheek to the smiter."

The United States called out an army of 15,000 men for purposes of attack on the Niagara frontier, and commanded General Wadsworth—of course, on paper—"to feed and cherish them." How well he executed this command remains to be seen.

What of Canada? Her yeomen forsook ploughshare and broadaxe, seized sword and musket, and rallied to the standard of Brock. In Upper Canada there was an active force of 950 regulars and marines and 550 militia. This little army had to defend the seven forts of Kingston, York, George, Erie, Chippewa, Amherstburg, and St. Joseph, not one of which was a fortress of strength, to patrol the lakes and protect a most vulnerable frontier. It was the opinion of leading military authorities that Canada could never be held against such an enemy.

Brock was at York when the news reached him. He at once sent part of the 41st to Niagara by lake, crossing

The United States of America Declares War

himself with his brigade-major, Evans, and Macdonell and Glegg, his aides, and, as usual, in a batteau, with eleven men. At Fort George he bade adieu to some American officers, guests of the mess, and sent them across the river. He was eager to storm Fort Niagara, whose capture might have changed the entire situation, but alas! what of his instructions?

He called out more militia, though he had only a few tents and many of the men were drilling without shoes. One hundred Tuscaroras under Chief Brant answered his summons. He divided his augmented Niagara force into four divisions—at Fort Erie 400 men, at Fort Chippewa 300, at Queenston 300, at Fort George 500. Of these, 900 were militia.

The rattle of the matchlock was as familiar as cockcrow. Every man became in fact, if not in deed, a volunteer. If the musket was not strapped to the tail of the plough, it leaned against the snake-fence—loaded. The goose-step, the manual and platoon took the place of the quadrille. Every clearing became a drill-hall, every log cabin an armoury. Many of the militia were crack shots, with all the scouting instincts of the forest ranger. In the barrack-square, in scarlet, white and green, the regulars drilled and went through wondrous evolutions with clock-work precision—fighting machinery with the tenacity of the bull-dog, though lacking the craft of the woods that had taught the volunteer the value of shelter and the wisdom of dwelling on his aim.

Apart, stolid and silent, but interested spectators, lounged the dusky redmen, forever sucking at their *pwoighun-ahsin* (stone pipes) and making tobacco from

The Story of Isaac Brock

the inner bark of red-willow wands, watching and wondering. The foot soldiers carried fire-locks, flints and cartridge boxes. These smooth-bore flint-locks had an effective range of less than 100 yards, and could be discharged only once a minute. Very different to the modern magazine rifle, which can discharge twenty-five shots in a minute and kill at 4,200 yards, while within 2,000 yards it is accurate and deadly. The mounted men were armed with sabres and ponderous pistols.

Our hero addressed the militia. The enemy, he told them, intended to lay waste the country. " Let them be taught," he said, " that Canadians would never bow their necks to a foreign yoke." As the custodian of their rights, he was trying to preserve all they held dear. He looked to them to repel the invaders.

Brock was placed in a most peculiar position, for while the passive Prevost was still instructing him—nearly three weeks *after* the declaration of war—" to take no offensive measures, as none would be taken by the United States Government," General Hull, with a force of 2,500 tried soldiers, was on his way from Ohio through the Michigan forests to occupy Detroit and invade Canada. Hull reached Detroit, and four days later, with his entire command, crossed the river and occupied Sandwich. But the trip was attended with serious mishap to his army, for Lieutenant Roulette, of the British sloop *Hunter*—a brother of the famous fur-trader—in a small batteau, with only six men, captured the United States packet *Cayuga,* with a detachment of five officers and thirty-three soldiers, as she was coming up the river. The *Cayuga's* treasure consisted not only of valuable stores and baggage,

The United States of America Declares War

but Hull's official correspondence with the United States Secretary of War. The contents of this decided Brock, though he had no idea Hull's army was so strong, to attempt the reduction of Fort Detroit without a moment's delay.

The very hour he knew that war was declared he had notified the officer at St. Joseph. Our hero, whose root idea of a soldier's craft was " secrecy in conception and vigour in execution," had no taste for Prevost's mad doctrine that the aggressed had to await the convenience of the aggressor. Brock had been taught to regard tolerance in war as an " evil of the first magnitude," and so had already instructed the commander at St. Joseph that if war was proclaimed he was to attack Mackinaw at once, but if attacked, " defend your post to the last." Prevost at the same time had ordered this officer " in case of necessity to effect his own retreat," never dreaming he would dare attack Mackinaw. What a contrast the despatches of these two men present! The one full of confidence, fight and resistance, the other shrinking from action and suggesting retreat. Brock's despatch was of later date and more palatable to the fighter at St. Joseph. He started at once for Mackinaw, fifty-five miles distant, with 45 of the 10th Royal veterans, 180 Canadians, many of whom were traders and voyageurs, and convoyed by the brig *Caledonia,* owned by the North-West Fur Company.

He landed before daybreak. By noon of that day the Union Jack was floating above the basalt cliffs of the Gibraltar of the north, and also over two of the enemy's vessels laden with furs. It is not on record that Captain Roberts was recommended by General Sir George Prevost

The Story of Isaac Brock

for promotion! The Indians at Amherstburg were now ready to support the British. Foremost among these was the great Shawanese warrior, Tecumseh.

General Hull, having meantime billeted himself in Colonel Baby's big brick house at Sandwich, issued a proclamation to the "inhabitants of Canada." As a sample of egotism, bluff and bombast it stands unrivalled. He told the inhabitants of Canada that he was in possession of their country, that an ocean and wilderness isolated them from England, whose tyranny he knew they felt. His grand army was ready to release them from oppression. They must choose between liberty and security, as offered by the United States, and war and annihilation, the penalty of refusal. He also threatened instant destruction to any Canadian found fighting by the side of an Indian, though General Dearborn, in command of the United States forces at Niagara, had been authorized by the United States Secretary of War "to organize the warriors of the Seneca Indians" *for active service against Canada.*

The United States Secretary of War wrote to Hull, saying his action respecting Canadian Indians "met with the approval of the Government." Evidently ashamed, upon reflection, of Hull's threat, that same Government later instructed its commissioners at the Treaty of Ghent, when peace was restored, "to disown and disavow" their former Indian policy.

Hull's extraordinary production, which proved a boomerang, was really the work of Colonel Lewis Cass, his Chief of Staff; but while Hull and Cass were "unloading their rhetoric at Sandwich," our hero was "loading his guns at Mackinaw."

Brock Accepts Hull's Challenge

CHAPTER XV.

BROCK ACCEPTS HULL'S CHALLENGE.

WITH the country's call for a saviour had arisen the man so sorely needed. Vigilant, sagacious and brave, but with most inadequate forces, Brock, faced by a crisis, hurried to repel the invasion by Hull. If Canada was to be saved, Detroit, as well as Mackinaw, must be reduced. The confidence also of the savages must be retained. The smallness of his army demanded the neutrality of the redmen, if not their active aid.

The plan of his campaign was laid before his Executive Council and the members of his staff. As they parted at the door of the General's quarters at midnight, preceding the day on which their gallant leader issued his counter reply to Hull, his final words were: "To hold Amherstburg, gentlemen, is of vital importance. It is the western base from which we must resist attack and advance upon Detroit. It must be held in force."

Brock's written answer to Hull's flamboyant address— edited by his wise adviser, Judge Powell—was eloquent and dignified. Hull's invitation to Canadians to seek protection from Britain under the flag of the United States was, he said, "an insult." He cited the advantages of British connection, and warned the colonists that secession meant the restitution of Canada to the Empire of France. This was the price to be paid by America for the aid given by France to the revolting States during

The Story of Isaac Brock

the War of Independence. He reminded them of the constancy of their fathers. " Are you prepared to become slaves to this despot Napoleon, who rules Europe with a rod of iron? If not, arise, repel the invader and give your children no cause to reproach you with sacrificing the richest inheritance of earth, participation in the name, character and freedom of Britons."

He told them not to be dismayed by the enemy's threat to " refuse them quarter should an Indian appear in their ranks." " Why," he continued, " should the brave bands of Indians which now inhabit this colony be prevented from defending their new homes?" These poor people, he reminded them, had actually been punished for their former fidelity to the United States, by the Government of that country taking from them their old homes in Ohio. The King of England had granted them a refuge and given them superior lands in Canada. Why were they to be denied the right to defend their hearths " from invasion by ferocious foes," who, while utilizing Indians themselves, had condemned the practice in others? The threat to refuse quarter to these defenders of invaded rights would, he said, bring about inevitable reprisal, for " the national character of Britain was not less distinguished for humanity than retributive justice."

The obstacles surrounding Brock would have driven an ordinary man to distraction. It is not possible to recite a fraction of them. The Grand River Indians, having received a specious letter from Hull, refused to join the relief expedition for Moraviantown, on the Thames, on which some of Hull's freebooters were marching. Some of the militia declined to leave their homes, suspicious,

Brock Accepts Hull's Challenge

they said, of Indian treachery. Some, with blood relations
in the States, refused point blank to take up arms. Others
were busy harvesting, while not a few came out openly as
traitors and joined the ranks of Hull. Brock had no
reinforcements of regular troops, and small chance of
getting any, and, what was far worse, he received little
moral support even from the Legislature, and none from
other sources from which he had a right to expect it. He
called an extra session of the House to enact laws to meet
the crisis, to invest him with greater authority and to
vote money for defence. He closed his Speech from the
Throne with a declaration delivered in sonorous, ringing
tones that echoed throughout the chamber:

"We are engaged in an awful and eventful contest.
By unanimity and vigour we may teach the enemy this
lesson, that a country defended by free men, devoted to
the cause of their King and constitution, can never be
conquered."

Though Brock's speech "inspired the faithful and
foiled the designs of some of the faithless," his demands
were conceded in part only, and he left for Fort George
with heart filled with misgivings. In answer to his request,
Prevost declined to define the extent of the authority with
which he had himself vested him. Extreme measures,
he told him, must be taken at his own risk. Our hero
was one of those limited few who had sounded the depths
of the truth that it was easier to do one's duty than to
know it. His shrewdness and self-reliance came to the
rescue. Seeing that the Niagara River would be selected
as the point for invasion, he made it his *defensive* frontier,
while the Detroit River was the *offensive* front of his

The Story of Isaac Brock

campaign. These views he outlined to his staff on the night following the prorogation of the House.

Judge Powell, after a long session of Council, the last to depart, was rising to leave. "Then, sir," said Colonel Macdonell, General Brock's new provincial aide, the young and brilliant Attorney-General of Upper Canada—engaged to Mary Powell, the daughter of the judge—"you really believe we can bombard Detroit successfully? The fort has, I understand, parapets twenty feet high, with four bastions, surrounded by palisades, a ditch and a glacis, and is capable of withstanding a long siege; besides which it has 2,500 fighting men to defend it."

"My good Macdonell," responded our hero, interest and deep regard imprinted on his face, "we fortunately know from Hull's own letters that he has as little confidence in his army as they have confidence in him. I fancy he is merely whistling to keep up his courage. A bold front on our part, with a judicious display of our small force, will give him cause to reflect. Then, provided we enthuse the Indians—and if Mackinaw is fallen, this should not be difficult—Detroit is ours!"

"How about Amherstburg and Sandwich, General?" interjected Justice Powell. "Their safety is essential to your plan."

"As to Amherstburg," said Brock, "it is the pivot point, sir, and must be retained as our base. At Sandwich we already have earthworks completed. If destroyed by Hull they must be rebuilt, for the batteries there must cover our crossing and cannonade the fort while we advance upon it. I have already sent, as you know, a few additional men to Procter—every man I can steal

Brock Accepts Hull's Challenge

from here. He should be able to hold his own at Amherstburg for a bit longer. The conditions, I admit, are far from satisfactory under the present command, but Chambers is on his way with forty of the 41st, one hundred militia with Merritt, and some of Brant's braves, to put backbone into the garrison."

"General," said Justice Powell, the rays from a waning moon flooding the hall-way as the outer door was opened by Brock for the exit of his councillors, "having implicit confidence in your judgment and military ability, I believe you will overthrow Hull. Assuming that you capture old Fort Lernoult and seize Detroit, what then?"

"What then, sir?" said Brock—emphasizing his parting words with a gesture of his hand—"why, Detroit taken, I shall return here, batter Fort Niagara—providing Prevost consents—and then by a sudden movement I could sweep the frontier from Buffalo to Fort Niagara and complete the salvation of Canada by the occupation of Sackett's Harbor. Good-night, gentlemen. *En avant, Detroit!*"

The Story of Isaac Brock

CHAPTER XVI.

"EN AVANT, DETROIT!"

UNDER an August moon Lake Erie shone as a shield of silver. Brock, with a fleet of small craft, batteaux and boats of every kind given him by the settlers, had pulled out from Long Point with 40 regulars and 260 militia for the relief of Amherstburg, two hundred miles distant.

The news of the fall of Mackinaw and the official declaration of war had only reached him as Parliament rose. He had proclaimed martial law before leaving York. He had also heard details of the attack by Hull's raiders on the Moravian settlement, sixty miles up the Thames. He knew of the repulse of 300 United States troops in three attempts to cross the Canard River bridge for an attack on Amherstburg, and of their being driven into the open plains, with loss, by Procter's men.

It was in one of these attacks that the first scalp in the war of 1812 was taken—not by one of Brock's terrible Indians, whose expected excesses had been referred to by Hull, but by a captain of Hull's spies. This officer —one hates to describe him as a white man—wrote his wife, he "had the pleasure of tearing a scalp from the head of a British redskin," and related at length the brutal details of his methods. They were those of a wild beast. "The first stroke of the tomahawk," Hull had stated in his proclamation, "the first attempt with the scalping-knife, will be the signal of a scene of desolation." Yet the first scalp taken in the Detroit campaign was by one of his own officers!

92

"En Avant, Detroit!"

Brock knew that the valorous Hull, dismayed at the advance of the British, had recrossed the river with all but 250 of his men and was hard at work on the defences of Fort Shelby, behind which he had retired. Brock also knew of the affair at Brownstown, where the Indian chief Tecumseh, with twenty-five warriors, had separated himself from Major Muir's detachment, sent to intercept a transport on its way from Ohio to Detroit with supplies for Hull. He had been told of the stratagem by which the great Shawanese warrior had ambushed the 200 American soldiers, near the Raisin River, who had marched from Detroit to escort this convoy and the mails. Seven American officers were killed at the Raisin, twelve of all ranks wounded, and seventy reported missing after the fight. In addition to the provision train, Tecumseh captured what was of much greater importance, another batch of Hull's despondent despatches. It was here that swift justice overtook the scalping Captain McCullough, of Hull's spies, who himself met with the fate of his former victim—the fate he deserved.

Brock also received despatches describing the daring attack by Lieutenant Roulette, of the provincial marine, who in a small boat with a handful of men had boarded and seized in the Detroit River a brigade of eleven batteaux! These, loaded with food, were on their way from Black Rock, and now carried fifty-six wounded American soldiers and two English prisoners. This bold feat of " cutting out " took place under the eyes of an armed escort of 250 American soldiers marching along the river bank.

Messengers from Procter had also informed Brock of the fight at Maguagua, fourteen miles below Detroit. It

The Story of Isaac Brock

was here that Muir, with 200 regulars and militia and less than 200 Indians, instead of waiting to be attacked, recklessly assailed a force of 600 Americans who were halted on the edge of the oak forest, supported by two six-pounder guns. Fighting without hope against such odds, the British were outflanked, Muir himself wounded, and an officer killed—the second British soldier to fall in the war of 1812. The American loss was eighteen killed and sixty-three wounded. Though the difference in arms and men was greatly in favour of the Americans, the British were enabled to retreat to the river, where they regained their boats. The American force, suffering from greater casualties, did not attempt to follow them.

Apart from the inferior strength of the British, the chief cause of their reverse at Maguagua was the blunder of some men of the 41st, who fired upon a body of Tecumseh's Indians. In rushing from the woods the redmen were mistaken for the enemy, and falling into a similar error themselves, they returned with interest the fire of the British soldiers. The disorder that followed created a panic. While Tecumseh with his own Indians fought bravely, the seventy Lake Indians under Caldwell suffered from "chill" and fled at the first shot. The most encouraging of these facts, when told to the expedition, aroused in Brock's followers a wild desire to meet Hull's army in battle.

Our hero's trip from Long Point was full of peril and hardship. The lake shore in places was extremely rugged. Precipitous cliffs of red clay and sun-baked sand rose two hundred feet from the boulder-strewn coast. Scarcely a creek offered shelter. The weather was unusually stormy. A heavy surf boomed on the shore. Flocks of water-fowl

"En Avant, Detroit!"

were driven before the wind. The men were drenched by torrents of rain. Though thirty miles in twenty-four hours was considered the maximum distance for rowing a batteau, nothing could retard this strange armada or dampen the confidence of the men in their resolute leader, who in an open boat led the way. In this boat, which was "headquarters," were Brock and his two aides. A lighted flambeau at the bow acted as a beacon during the night. After five days of great vigilance and galley-slave work, the toilers reached Amherstburg. Without the help of these hardy and resourceful men of the Canadian militia this trip could not have been accomplished.

The conduct of these bold frontiersmen aroused Brock's admiration. His own example had again acted as an inspiration. Shortly after leaving Port Talbot, his batteau, pounding in the sea, ran upon a reef that extended far from shore, and despite oars and pike-poles, remained fast. In the height of the confusion "Master Isaac" sprang overboard, and a moment later voyageur and raw recruit, waist deep in water, following the example of the hero of Castle Cornet, lifted the batteau over the dangerous ledge.

When at midnight the boats passed up the Strait— through which the ambitious La Salle and Father Hennepin had passed in 1679—and grated on the gravel beach at Amherstburg, Brock was greeted with a volley of musketry by the Indians. This was contrary to his rigid rubric of war. Such waste of powder must not be tolerated. He turned to the Indian superintendent, " Do pray, Colonel Elliott," said he, " explain my reasons for objecting to the firing and tell the Chiefs I will talk with them to-morrow."

The Story of Isaac Brock

CHAPTER XVII.

OUR HERO MEETS TECUMSEH.

A FEW minutes only had elapsed when Elliott returned. The sentry's challenge caused Brock to look up from the table, littered with plans and despatches. Another figure darkened the doorway.

" This, sir," said Elliott, " is Tecumseh, the Shawanese chief of whom you have heard, and who desires to be presented to you."

The General, who had removed the stains of travel and was in uniform, rose to his full height, bowed, extended his hand and explained in manly fashion the reason for asking that the firing be stopped. The contrast presented by the two men was striking. The old world and the new, face to face—a scene for the brush of an impressionist. Brock, tall, fair, big-limbed, a blue-eyed giant, imposing in scarlet coat and blue-white riding trousers, tasselled Hessian boots, and cocked-hat in hand. On his benevolent face was an irresistible smile.

The Indian, though of middle height, was of most perfect proportions, an athlete in bronze, lithe and supple as a panther. His oval face, set in a frame of glistening black hair, shone like a half-polished copper relief. Overlooking the nose, straight as one of his own arrows, and from which some tinkling silver coins were suspended, a pair of hawk-like eyes, hazel-black and unflinching—in which the secrets of the world seemed slumbering—

OUR HERO MEETS TECUMSEH. "THIS IS A MAN!"

Our Hero Meets Tecumseh

gleamed upon Brock. His dress, a hunting jacket of tanned deer-skin and close-fitting leggings. Fringed mocassins of the same material, richly embroidered in silk and porcupine quills dyed in divers colours, encased his feet. The light from the open log fire flickered fitfully, half revealing the antlered heads of moose and caribou and other trophies of the chase that, hanging from the rafters, looked down upon the group, adding weirdness to the picture.

Brock briefly explained that he had come to fight the King's enemies, enemies who so far had never seen his back, and who were Tecumseh's enemies also. " Would Tecumseh maintain an honourable warfare ?"

Perhaps no eulogy of Brock was ever penned that so well summed up his qualities as did the terse, four-worded certificate of character uttered by the Indian before replying to the British general's appeal. Tecumseh looked " Master Isaac's " commanding physique up and over, over and down—Brock's caution as to waste of powder doubtless weighing with him—until eye met eye, and then, impulsively extending his thin brown hand, turned to his followers, exclaiming in tones of highest admiration:

" *This* is a man !"

Assenting " Ughs " and " Ho-hos " followed in rapid succession, and in response to Brock's invitation the headmen, painted and plumed and in striped blankets, squatted on their stained reed mats and wild-beast skins on the basswood log floor. Questioned as to the nature of the country westward, Tecumseh took a roll of elm-bark and with the point of his scalping-knife traced on its white inner surface the features of the region—hills, forests, trails, rivers,

97

The Story of Isaac Brock

muskegs and clearings. Rough, perhaps, but as accurate, he said, as if drawn by a pale-face *teebahkeè-wayninni* (surveyor).

That night, after Tecumseh's return, Brock again held council with his staff, proposing an attack on Detroit. Only one of his chief officers, the staunch colonial quartermaster, Lieutenant-Colonel Nichol, agreed with him. Colonel Henry Procter, from whom he had expected whole-hearted support, strongly objected. History teaches us that the conception of a daring plan is the offspring of great minds only. Procter was not of this class, as his subsequent record shows. Some of our hero's critics have described his resolve to attack Detroit as " audacious and desperate." Isaac Brock was, of course, nothing if not contemptuously daring. The greater the difficulty that faced him the more was he determined to challenge the obstacle, that to a less confident man would have been rejected as insurmountable. He had, however, resolved and planned not only upon taking Detroit, but, if need be, the pursuit and capture of Hull's entire army, compelling him to either stand and fight or surrender. With habitual prescience he had weighed well the issues and chosen the lesser alternative. His own defeat and possibly his death, on the one hand, against the probable salvation of half a continent on the other. What true soldier could hesitate ?

While patiently hearing objections, he brushed the most of them aside as mere flies on the wheel. Surely the way had been opened to him. The seized despatches had revealed the discord among Hull's troops and shown him that while the United States militia, the flower of Ohio

Our Hero Meets Tecumseh

and Kentucky, was of good material, the United States soldiers were not. He knew that the situation in Upper Canada called for extreme measures, and that the time to strike was now or never, for his scouts had truly reported that 350 United States mounted troops were pressing close upon his rear. They were, in fact, only a mile or two distant. If his own inferior force was out-flanked, or his communication with the Canadian interior cut, it spelled utter disaster. He was in a wilderness without hope of reinforcements. As Colonel Cass, the United States commander, later reported to the President, Brock was "between two fires and with no hope of succour." Brock knew he must act at once or even retreat might be impossible. With inborn acumen he saw at a glance the peril of his own position, and with cool courage hastened to avert it. He realized that upon the " destruction or discomfiture " of Hull's forces " the safety of the province depended."

Brock listened closely to Procter's argument—by this time he knew, of course, that Hull's own line of communication with his reserves had been cut—then rising, when all who cared to speak had finished, he said: " Gentlemen, I have definitely decided on crossing the river and attacking Fort Detroit. Instead of further advice I must beg of you to give me your hearty support. The general orders for to-morrow will be issued at once."

This decision was typical of the man of action. " Prudent only where recklessness was a fault, and hazardous only when hesitation meant defeat."

The Story of Isaac Brock

CHAPTER XVIII.

AN INDIAN POW-WOW.

IT was a picturesque council of white men and Indians that was held at dawn in an open glade of the forest. The fragrant odours of the bush mingled with the pungent smoke of the red willow-bark, puffed from a hundred pipes. Conspicuous at this pow-wow was Tecumseh, who across his close-fitting buckskin hunting jacket, which descended to his knees and was trimmed with split leather fringe, wore a belt of wampum, made of the purple enamel of mussel shells—cut into lengths like sections of a small pipe-stem, perforated and strung on sinew. On his head he wore a toque of eagle plumes.

"My object," said Brock, addressing the Indians, " is to assist you to drive the ' Long-knives ' [Americans] from the frontier, and repel invasion of the King's country." Tecumseh, speaking for his tribesmen, remarked, not without sarcasm, that " their great father, King George, having awakened out of a long sleep, they were now ready to shed their last drop of blood in that father's service."

"The pale faces," he continued, after an impressive pause—and the fire of his eloquence and his gestures swayed his hearers like the reeds on the river bank— "the Americans who want to fight the British are our enemies. . . . They came to us hungry and they cut off the hands of our brothers who gave them corn. . . . We gave them rivers of fish and they poisoned our foun-

An Indian Pow-wow

tains. . . . We gave them forest-clad mountains and valleys full of game, and in return what did they give our warriors and our women? Rum and trinkets and— a grave! . . . The shades of our fathers slaughtered on the banks of the Tippecanoe can find no rest. . . . Their eyes can see no herds on the hills of light in the hunting grounds of the dead! . . . Until our enemies are no more we must be as one man, under one chief, whose name is—Death! . . . I have spoken."

Tecumseh, it should be known, bore a personal grudge against the Americans, especially against the 4th Regiment, then in garrison at Detroit, the "heroes of Tippecanoe." This was a terrible misnomer, for under General Harrison, with 1,000 soldiers, less than a year before, they had taken part in the slaughter of Tecumseh's half-armed band of 600 men and women on the banks of the Tippecanoe River, during that chief's absence with many of his warriors, and had laid waste his village. With a perhaps pardonable spirit of vindictiveness, such as is shared by both redskin and white man, the human-being in him thirsted for revenge.

Brock, perceiving Tecumseh's sagacity and influence over the savages, invited the Shawanese and Wawanosh, Ojebekun and the other sachems, to a private council. Here he unfolded his plans. Before doing this he made it a condition that no barbarities were to be committed. "The scalping-knife," said he, "must be discarded, and forbearance, compassion and clemency shown to the vanquished." He told them he wanted to restrict their military operations to the known rules of war, as far as was possible under the singular conditions in which they

The Story of Isaac Brock

fought, and exacted a promise from the lofty-minded Tecumseh that his warriors "should not taste pernicious liquor until they had humbled the Big-knives." "If this resolution," remarked Brock, "is persevered in, you must surely conquer."

Brock's rapid ascendency over the Indians was astonishing; they already revered him as a common father.

That same afternoon our hero, moving up with his entire command to Sandwich, occupied the mansion of Colonel Baby, the great fur-trader, just evacuated by Hull. In the spacious hall hooks were nailed to the rafters, from which were suspended great steel-yards, by which the beaver packs were weighed. Scattered on the hewn floor in much profusion were soldiers' accoutrements, service and pack-saddles, iron-bound chests mixed up with bear-traps and paddles, rolls of birch-bark, leather hunting shirts, and the greasy blankets of voyageur and redskin. The room on the right became Brock's headquarters, and in this room he penned his first demand upon General Hull.

"My force," so he wrote, "warrants my demanding the immediate surrender of Fort Detroit." Anxious to prevent bloodshed, and knowing Hull's dread of the Indians, he also played upon his fears. "The Indians," he added, "might get beyond my control." This summons was carried by Colonel Macdonell and Major Glegg, under a flag of truce, across the river.

The batteries at Sandwich consisted of one eighteen-pounder, two twelve-pounders, and two 5½-inch howitzers. Back of these artificial breastworks extended both a wilderness and the garden of Canada. Beyond the meadows,

An Indian Pow-wow

aflame with autumn wild-flowers, beyond the cultivated clearings, rose a forest of walnut, oak, basswood, birch and poplar trees, seared with age, of immense height and girth, festooned with wild honeysuckle and other creepers. In the open were broad orchards bending under their harvest of red and yellow fruit—apples and plums, peaches, nectarines and cherries—and extensive vineyards. Huge sugar maples challenged giant pear trees, whose gnarled trunks had resisted the storms of a century. To the north the floor of the forest was interlaced with trails, which, with the intention of deceiving Hull's spies as to the strength of Brock's forces, had been crossed and recrossed, and countermarched and doubled over, by the soldiers and Tecumseh's half-naked braves.

The air was filled with the fragrance of orchard and forest. Facing our hero, flowed the river, broad, swift and deep; tufted wolf-willow, waving rushes and gray hazel fringing the banks. Across and beyond this almost mile-wide ribbon of water, the imposing walls of Fort Detroit confronted him. Approaching him at a rapid gait he at last espied his two despatch bearers, their scarlet tunics vivid against the green background. They reported that, after waiting upon Hull for two hours without being granted an interview, they were handed the following reply:

"General Hull is prepared to meet any force brought against him, and accept any consequences."

Brock instructed his gunners to acknowledge the receipt of this challenge with the thunder of their batteries, and from then, far into the night, shells and round-shot shrieked their way across the river, the answering missiles from

The Story of Isaac Brock

Hull's seven twenty-four-pounders breaking in a sheet of flame from the very dust created by the British cannon-balls that exploded on the enemy's breastworks. Through the irony of fate, the first shot fired under Brock's personal orders in the cause of Canadian freedom killed a United States officer, an intimate friend of the British artilleryman who had trained the gun. Such are the arguments of war.

The cannonade proving ineffective, as judged by visible results, Brock issued orders to cross the river at dawn, when he would make the attempt to take the fort by storm —and soldier and militiaman bivouacked on their arms.

.   .   .   .

Camp fires were extinguished, but the tireless fireflies danced in the blackness of the wood. The river gurgled faintly in the wind-stirred reeds. From out the gloom of the thicket came the weird *coco-coco* of the horned owl. From the starlit sky above fell the shrill cry of the mosquito hawk, " *peepeegeeceese, peepeegeeceese!*" From an isolated bark tepee came the subdued incantation of the Indian medicine-man, while above the singing of the tree-tops and over all, clear and with clock-like regularity, floated the challenge of the sentry and answering picket:

" Who goes there ?"

" A friend."

" All's well."

The Attack on Detroit

CHAPTER XIX.

THE ATTACK ON DETROIT.

MORNING came all too slowly for Brock's impatient soldiers. At last the *reveille* warned the expectant camp. The sun rose, a red-hot shell out of the faint August haze, huge and threatening. With its advent the British batteries resumed their fire, aided by the guns on the *Queen Charlotte* and *Hunter,* which lay in the river, above the village known to-day as Windsor, to cover the embarkation of the troops in batteaux and canoes.

Brock's entire force consisted of only 330 regulars and 400 militia, some of whom, acting on a happy thought, were disguised in discarded uniforms of the 41st. This army was supported by five pieces of artillery. All crossed the river in safety, landing at Spring Wells, four miles below. The Indians, 600 strong, under Tecumseh, in addition to the men of his own nation, consisted of many Sioux, Wyandottes and Dacotahs. The majority of these crossed under cover of the night. History records no instance of a determined force being stopped by a river. The Detroit River presented an animated picture. Edging their way through a maze of boats and batteaux, and in marked contrast to the scarlet-coated soldiers and blue-shirted sailors, bark canoes on which were drawn in flaring colours a variety of barbaric designs, flitted here and there, their crews of half-naked savages fearsome in fresh war-paint and gaudy feathers. Coo-ees, shrieks and

The Story of Isaac Brock

shrill war-whoops—" Ah-oh! Ah-oo!" like the dismal yells
of a pack of coyotes—rent the air, the discordant din ever
and anon drowned by the thunder of the guns from the
Sandwich batteries.

Upon landing Brock mustered his men. The reports
showed 750 of all ranks, including the voyageurs left in
charge of the river squadron. The 600 Indians deployed
in the shelter of the woods, skirmishing to effect a flank
movement. The column, having formed, was moved forward in sections, and at double distance, to lend a fictitious
air of strength; the light artillery, of three, six, and two
three-pounders, being immediately in rear of the advance
guards, the whole preceded by fluttering standards and
rolling drums. Three generations ago! Yet you can see
it all to-day as plainly as Brock saw it, if you but close
your eyes and conjure up the past.

The enemy, over 2,000 strong, drawn up in line upon
an overlooking rise, had planted in the roadway, commanding the approach to the town, two twenty-four
pounders, each loaded with six dozen grapeshot, around
which the gunners stood with burning fuses, challenging
our hero's advance.

Up and down, in front of the line, rode Isaac Brock
on his gray charger, his brilliant uniform—khaki was
unknown in those days—flashing in the morning sun, a
shining mark. A command here, a kindly rebuke there,
a word of encouragement to all ranks; the eyes of Britain
and Canada were upon them; they might have to take
the fort by storm,—even so, honour and glory awaited
them. . . . Forward then, for King and country!

The rat-a-tat-tat of the kettle-drums, the clear-cut

106

The Attack on Detroit

whistle of the fifes, the resonant roll of the big drums, the steady tramp, tramp of armed men—and the human machine was in motion.

. . . .

The long grim guns on Fort Detroit and Hull's field-pieces pointed their black muzzles at the column. Up and down, in front of his men, rode Isaac Brock.

. . . .

Now this was more than some flesh and blood could stand. Spurring his horse, acting Quartermaster-General Nichol reined up alongside his beloved commander. "General," he said, saluting his leader, while the soldiers' faces expressed dumb approval, " forgive me, but I cannot forbear entreating you not to expose yourself. If we lose you, we lose all. I pray you, allow the troops to advance, led by their own officers."

"Master Nichol," said Brock, turning in his saddle and returning the salute of the gallant Quartermaster, " I fully appreciate your kindly advice, but I feel that, in addition to their sense of loyalty and duty, there are many here following me from a feeling of personal regard, and I will never ask them to go where I do not lead."

Before him spread the plain, broken here and there with *coulees* and clumps of bush. A partly fenced road-way, with some scattered houses on the river bank, but no barbed-wire entanglements, impeded his movements. The introduction of such pleasant devices was left for a higher civilization!

. . . .

The Story of Isaac Brock

The column was in motion. The steady onward tramp, tramp of this thin red line, raw recruit and grizzly veteran shoulder to shoulder, struck fear into the heart of the unfortunate Hull. The prospect, though his troops outnumbered the British three to one, was clearly war to the knife. Brock's meaning was apparent. Should he or should he not accept the Englishman's challenge? He could extract no comfort out of that solid scarlet front, bristling with naked steel, now fast approaching in battle array with even, ominous tread.

.   .   .   .

The siege-proof walls of the fort lay behind him. His irresolute heart grew faint, and in the flash of a flintlock in its pan, honour was sacrificed and fame cast to the winds. A brave army of martyrs, over 2,000 strong, was rightabout faced, and drinking the cup of humiliation, that only men of courage can drain to the bitter dregs, this army, eager to lock bayonets with the British, was tually ordered to retreat into the shelter of Fort Detroit!

From a Silhouette in possession of John Alexander Macdonell, K.C., Alexandria

LIEUTENANT-COLONEL JOHN MACDONELL.

Provincial Aid-de-Camp to Major-General Sir Isaac Brock ; M.P. for Glengarry ;
Attorney-General of Upper Canada.

Brock's Victory

CHAPTER XX.

BROCK'S VICTORY.

REACHING a ravine, Brock ordered up his artillery and prepared to assault. A shell from the British battery at Sandwich roared over the river and crashed through an embrasure of Fort Shelby, killing four American officers. The Savoyard river was reached and the outlying tan-yard crossed. Brock's troops, keyed up, with nerves tense under the strain of suspense, and every moment expecting a raking discharge of shot and shell from the enemy's big guns, heard with grim satisfaction the General's orders to " prepare for assault."

The field-pieces were trained upon the fort, to cover the rush of the besiegers. The gunners, with bated breath and burning fuses, awaited the final command, when lo! an officer bearing a white flag emerged from the fort, while a boat with another flag of truce was seen crossing the river to the Sandwich battery. Macdonell and Glegg galloped out to meet the messenger. They returned with a despatch from the American general, Hull, to the British general, Brock. This was the message:

" The object of the flag which crossed the river was to propose a cessation of hostilities for an hour, for the purpose of entering into negotiations for the surrender of Detroit."

. . . .

An hour later the British troops, with General Isaac

The Story of Isaac Brock

Brock at their head, marched through the smiling fields and orchards, passed over the fort draw-bridge, and, surrounded by a host of fierce-looking and indignant militia of Ohio and "the heroes of Tippecanoe," hauled down the Stars and Stripes—which had waved undisturbed over Fort Lernoult since its voluntary evacuation by the British in 1796—and, in default of a British ensign, hoisted a Union Jack—which a sailor had worn as a body-belt—over the surrendered fortress. British sentinels now guarded the ramparts. The bells of old St. Anne's saluted the colors. The "Grand Army of the West," by which pretentious title Hull had seen fit to describe his invading force, melted like mist before the rising sun.

Several unattached Canadians, costumed as redmen, followed Brock inside the fort, and, baring their white arms for Hull's especial edification, declared they had so disguised themselves in order to show their contempt for his cruel threat respecting instant death to "Indians found fighting."

The terms of capitulation included not only one general officer and 2,500 men of all ranks—the would-be conquerors of Canada—2,500 stand of arms, 33 pieces of cannon, the *Adams* brig of war, and immense quantities of stores and munitions, valued at £40,000—but Fort Shelby and the town of Detroit and 59,700 square miles of United States territory. Nor were these all, for the fort standard—to the wild delight of Tecumseh's warriors —a highly-prized trophy, it being the "colours" of the 4th United States regiment, the vaunted "heroes of Tippecanoe," passed into the keeping of the British.

Canada was saved!

Brock's Victory

It was then that those officers who strongly opposed Brock's determination to attack became suddenly wise after the event and eager to share the honour. The temptation to improve the opportunity, to any man less strong than our hero, would have been irresistible, but there was no display of vainglory, no cheap boasting. The sword of the conquered American general was accepted with manly deference and the consideration due to his rank, and he was told, without solicitation on his part, he could return to the United States on parole. Then Brock hurriedly dictated a brief and modest despatch apprising Sir George Prevost of the " capture of this very important post," and quite realizing that he was merely an instrument in the hands of Providence, and gratitude and the happiness of those he held most dear being uppermost in his mind, the captor of Detroit wrote this characteristic letter.

" Headquarters, Detroit,
" August 16, 1812.

" My dear Brothers and Friends,—Rejoice at my good fortune and join me in prayers to heaven. I send you a copy of my hasty note to Sir George. Let me know that you are all united and happy.

" ISAAC."

And so it came about that in this strange and noble fashion General Brock—"Master Isaac of St. Peter's Port "—overcame the enemy in the wilds of Michigan and passed his *fourth* milestone.

The Story of Isaac Brock

CHAPTER XXI.

CHAGRIN IN THE UNITED STATES.

THE conduct of the Indians under Tecumseh at Detroit had been marked by great heroism and strict adherence to their pledges. "The instant the enemy submitted, his life became sacred." In recognition of Tecumseh's work, and in the presence of the troops formed in the fort square, Brock handed him his silver-mounted pistols, and taking off his sash, tied it round the body of the chief.

A suspicion of a smile—the faint smile of elation of the well-trained child accepting a prize—flitted across the Indian's finely chiselled face as, proudly inclining his head, he silently took the crimson band. Then unwinding his own parti-colored, closely-woven Red River belt, "Would the great white *shemogonis* (warrior)," he whispered, "accept the simple sash of the Shawanese in return?"

To this there was a sequel. The next day, when he bade Brock farewell, Tecumseh wore no sash. "Roundhead," he explained, "was an older, an abler warrior than himself. While he was present he could not think of wearing such a badge of distinction." He had given the sash to the Wyandotte chieftain. Tecumseh proved himself a greater diplomat than Hull.

The papers of surrender signed, Brock hastened to liberate Dean, a soldier of the 41st, wounded and taken prisoner at the Canard river, with another man, while

Chagrin in the United States

gallantly defending the bridge against a large body of the enemy. In a voice broken with emotion Brock told him that he had "nobly upheld the traditions of the service and was an honour to his profession." Then he singled out Lieutenant Roulette, of the sloop *Hunter*, a French Canadian, who captured eighteen prizes during the war and was the leading spirit in many gallant events. "I watched you during the action," said the General. "You behaved like a lion. I will remember you." In the orders of that afternoon Brock praised the conduct of his troops. He laid stress upon the "discipline and determination that had decided an enemy, infinitely more numerous in men and artillery, and protected by a strong fortification, to propose capitulation."

The effect of the news in Upper Canada was electrical. Brock became the idol of the people and was acclaimed "hero and saviour of Upper Canada." His performance was a record one. In nineteen days he had met the Legislature, settled important public business, transported a small army 300 miles, 200 of which was by open boat in stormy waters, compelled the surrender of an enemy three times his strength, entrenched in a protected fort, and seized 60,000 square miles of United States mainland and islands.

To the American people the news came as a thunderclap. President Madison's chagrin was indescribable. After all the insulting remarks and bombastic prophecies of himself and Clay, Calhoun, Eustis and others, the humiliation was as gall and wormwood. Clay, the apostate, later on swallowed his words and signed the treaty of peace. Eustis, the Secretary of War, had boasted that

113

The Story of Isaac Brock

he would " take the whole country and ask no favours, for God has given us the power and the means." But God saw fit to confound the despoiler. Hull was, of course, made a scapegoat. Tried by court-martial, he was found guilty of cowardice and neglect, and sentenced to death, but pardoned by the President. His son died fighting at Lundy's Lane. The officers of Hull's command, who were almost united in opposing surrender, as brave men felt their position keenly. Never let us forget that no one race holds a monopoly in courage, that no nation has exclusive control of the spirit of patriotism. Fortunate it is indeed for most of us that the loftier qualities of man can not be copyrighted by the individual. A share of these has been bestowed in wise proportion upon all members of the human family. To those who seek to emulate the character and deeds of the world's famous men, certain essential qualities of mind may even be acquired and developed by all, but to possess the " fullness of perfection " cannot be the lot of every man.

Having finished " the business " that took him to Detroit, our hero did not waste an hour. Leaving Procter in command, he started before morning of the next day for Fort George, anxious to carry out his plans and assume the offensive on the Niagara frontier.

He embarked in the *Chippewa,* a small trading schooner, with seventy of the Ohio Rifles as prisoners, and took, as a guard, a rifle company commanded by his young friend, Captain Robinson, subsequently Chief Justice Robinson, " again winning golden opinions from the men by his urbanity."

On Lake Erie he met the *Lady Prevost,* of fourteen

Chagrin in the United States

guns, the commander of which, after saluting the hero of Detroit with seventeen guns, boarded the *Chippewa,* handing him despatches that notified him of an *armistice,* which Sir George Prevost had actually concluded with the American general, Dearborn, on August 9th! Brock's mortification was profound. His cherished plan, to sweep the Niagara frontier and destroy the United States naval arsenal at Sackett's Harbour, was again frustrated.

A diversion occurred that morning which for a time drove the unpardonable armistice from Brock's thoughts. A heavy mist hung over the water. It hid the shore. Deceived by this, the skipper of the *Chippewa,* who thought he was in Fort Erie harbour, discovered, as the fog lifted, that they were on the American side and close to Buffalo. The situation was perilous and dramatic. With the melting of the haze the wind dropped. Brock saw on the Buffalo shore, within easy hail, a concourse of inquisitive people trying to make out the nationality of his ship. Believing the skipper was in league with the enemy, Brock turned upon him savagely.

"You scoundrel," said he, "you have betrayed me. Let but one shot be fired and I will run you up at the yard-arm." Fortunately, the *Queen Charlotte,* in Canadian water, was seen and signalled, and, the wind rising, she convoyed the *Chippewa* and her precious passenger into safety.

The news of the armistice dumbfounded the General. Instead of battering Fort Niagara and attacking Sackett's Harbour, he had to order Procter to cancel the expedition for the relief of Fort Wayne, in the Wabash country, and himself hurry on to Fort George. At Chippewa he was

The Story of Isaac Brock

received with wild welcome by the river residents and the populace from the countryside. A deputation of prominent men met him at Queenston, placed him in an open carriage, and with martial music he was escorted in triumph to Fort George. After receiving at Niagara the congratulations of the lady to whom he was engaged, Brock took schooner for York and Kingston. At both of these places fervid demonstrations were showered upon him. But "Master Isaac's" head could not be turned either by success or adulation. The old spirit of self-effacement asserted itself. "The gallant band of brave men," he said, "at whose head I marched against the enemy, are the proper objects of your gratitude. The services of the militia have been duly appreciated and will never be forgotten."

Isaac's modesty again served to increase the homage and profound devotion of the people.

Justice Powell voiced the views of the citizens of Upper Canada when he declared Brock could "boast of the most brilliant success, with the most inadequate means, which history records. . . . It was something fabulous that a handful of troops, supported by a few raw militia, could invade the country of an enemy of doubtful numbers, in his own fortress, and make all prisoners without the loss of a man."

"If this sort of thing lasts," commented our hero to a friend, "I am afraid I shall do some foolish thing, for if I know myself there is no want of what is called courage in my nature, and I can only hope I shall not be led into some scrape."

QUEENSTON HEIGHTS AND BROCK'S MONUMENT (Original painting by C. M. Manly, A.R.C.A.)

Prevost's Armistice

CHAPTER XXII.

PREVOST'S ARMISTICE:

THE armistice paralyzed Brock's movements. All the moral influence and material advantage gained by the captures of Mackinaw and Detroit were nullified by this incredible blunder, for which no reason, military or civil, has ever been assigned. The loyal volunteers were released from duty. Brock's Indian allies returned to their villages. Prevost's policy of peace had become a mental malady. In spite of our hero's pleadings, and though Prevost actually knew, before the fall of Detroit, that President Madison would not extend the two weeks' armistice, the Governor-General forbade Brock attacking either Sackett's Harbour, the key to American supremacy on the lakes, or Fort Niagara.

" War," wrote Prevost, " has never yet been declared by England. Peace is possible."

Brock, smarting under restraint and handcuffed by red tape, was compelled to look on while the enemy brought up reinforcements, powder, shot, provisions and other munitions of war, by water to Lewiston. General Van Rensselaer, in command of the American forces at Lewiston, wrote to the President stating that by " keeping up a bold front he had succeeded in getting from General Sheaffe at Fort George the uninterrupted use of the lakes and rivers." The strategic advantage to the enemy of this cessation of hostilities and the privileges conceded

The Story of Isaac Brock

was enormous. Prevost realized his error too late. The following year, conceiving it then to be his special mission to borrow our dead hero's policy, he attacked Sackett's Harbour, but his "cautious calculation" was, of course, rewarded by ignoble defeat, and ultimately, after the Plattsburg fiasco, by a court-martial. In his civil administration of Canada Sir George Prevost may have been a success; as a soldier he was a sad failure.

Isaac was daily proving the truth of the precept, recognized by all men sooner or later, that life's values lie not so much in its victories as in its strife.

Though Brock awoke after Detroit to find himself famous, and a hero whose prowess far exceeded that of his ancestor, the Jurat of the Royal Court of Guernsey, over whose exploits he used to ponder seated on the Lion's Rock at Cobo, he was still the same "Master Isaac," still the "beloved brother." Separation from his kinsmen only served to draw him closer.

Crossing Lake Ontario gave him the opportunity he longed for. He wrote to his brothers collectively, telling them the sundry details of his success, "which was beyond his expectation." He hoped the affair would meet with recognition at the War Office. Though admitting it was a desperate measure, he told them " it proceeded from a cool calculation of the *pros* and *cons*," and as Colonel Procter had opposed it, he was not surprised that envy now induced that officer " to attribute to good fortune what in reality was the result of my own knowledge and discernment." But praise and honours, though sweet to our hero, who after all was only mortal, were secondary to the fact that he would be in a position to contribute

Prevost's Armistice

something to the comfort and happiness of his brothers.
The value of the " treasure " captured at Detroit was
placed at £40,000. Brock's share of this was a substantial
sum.

" When I returned heaven thanks," he wrote, " for
my amazing success, I thought of you all, your late sor-
rows forgotten, and I felt that the many benefits which
for a series of years I received from you were not
unworthily bestowed." But the hope that they were
reunited was always the dominant note. " Let me know,
my dearest brothers," he pleaded, " that you are all again
united." Then, out of his own knowledge, wrought of
deep experience in the world's wide field, he proceeded:
" The want of union was nearly losing this province, without even a struggle; rest assured, it operates in the same
degree in regard to families."

Brock's despatches, with the story of the capture of
Detroit and the colours of the 4th Regiment, United States
Army, the oriflamme of the " heroes of Tippecanoe,"
reached London the morning of October 6th, the anniversary of his birth. His brother William resided close
to the city. A tumultuous clangour of bells and booming
of guns from St. James' Park and the Tower of London
rent the air. When asked by his wife the reason for the
jubilation he jokingly replied, " Why, for Isaac, of course.
You surely have not forgotten this is his birthday." But
William, on reaching the city, learned to his amazement
that his jesting words were true. The salvoes of artillery
and peals of bells were indeed in honour of General
Brock's victory in far-off Michigan.

Neither King nor Imperial Government was slow to

The Story of Isaac Brock

recognize our hero's achievements. The Prince Regent, who expressed his appreciation of Brock's "able, judicious and decisive conduct," bestowed upon him an *extra* knighthood of the Order of the Bath, in consideration, so ran the document, "of all the difficulties with which he was surrounded during the invasion of the Province, and the singular judgment, firmness, skill and courage with which he surmounted them so effectually."

When the glittering insignia of his new rank reached Canada, Sir Isaac Brock's eyes were closed in death. His inanimate body, from which one of the noblest souls of the century had fled, lay rigid in its winding-sheet at Fort George.

To Major Glegg, who bore the General's despatches from Canada, the Prince Regent remarked that "General Brock had done more in an hour than could have been done in six months by negotiation." The fulfilment of Isaac's favourite maxim, "Say and do," was being demonstrated in a most remarkable manner.

"MAJOR-GENERAL BROCK, 18 × 6."

(From miniature painting by J. Hudson.)

"Hero, Defender, Saviour"

CHAPTER XXIII.

"HERO, DEFENDER, SAVIOUR."

GENERAL SHEAFFE, the only field officer available, and junior colonel of the 49th, of whom the reader has already heard, had been brought from the East to take command at Niagara in Brock's absence. Like Prevost, he was born in Boston, Massachusetts, in 1763, a son of the deputy collector of that port. There the two had been school-fellows, and both found it difficult to engage in vigorous diplomatic or military conflict with the Americans. To Sheaffe's credit, it should be said that he applied for another station.

It was Sheaffe, however, who acceded to General Dearborn's specious demand that the *freedom of the lakes and rivers* be extended to the United States Government during the armistice. This was done while Brock was in the West. Sheaffe it also was who, with hat in hand and strange alacrity, later agreed, despite his first terrible blunder, to repeat the offence. On the very afternoon that the British defeated the Americans at Queenston, and when the moral effect of that victory, followed up by vigorous attack, would have saved Canada from a continuance of the war, and deplorable loss of life and trade, Sheaffe actually agreed to another armistice. For this *second* truce, like his first, "no valid reason, military or civil, has ever been assigned." As far as the British were concerned, neither of these two was necessary, but, on the

The Story of Isaac Brock

contrary, directly to their disadvantage. Isaac Brock, alas! was not made in duplicate.

Our hero remained but a few hours in Kingston. He was needed in Niagara. The enemy was burning to avenge Detroit. The sight of Hull's ragged legions passing as prisoners of war along the Canadian bank of the river, bound for Montreal, did not tend to soften the hearts of the Americans. Stores and ordnance continued to pour into Lewiston. Brock needed 1,000 additional regulars. He might as well have asked for the moon. Early in September he stated that if he could maintain his position six weeks longer "the campaign would end in a manner little expected in the States." Scores of American marines and seamen were marking time, waiting for the launching of the vessels which Captain Chauncey had been given free license to build to ensure United States supremacy of the lakes. Prevost's eyes were still bandaged. Brock warned his grenadiers of the 49th to be ready for trouble. He foresaw that the Niagara river would be crossed, but at what point was uncertain. Stray musket-balls whistled across at night as thick as whip-poor-wills in summer. This firing was "the unauthorized warfare between sentinels." The peaceful citizens of Newark, returning from dance or card-party—even the imminence of war did not wholly stifle their desire for innocent revelry—found it embarrassing.

Though Van Rensselaer's force now numbered 6,300 men, he was still afraid to attack Brock. Invited by the United States Government to take up arms, 400 Seneca Indians "went upon the war-path," and performed ghost-dances on the streets of Lewiston. Prevost, with no pro-

"Hero, Defender, Saviour"

per conception of the doctrine of " what we have we hold," ordered Brock to " evacuate Detroit and the territory of Michigan." To " the man behind the gun," who had but just donated this 60,000 square miles of realty to the Empire, such instructions were hardly to his taste. Armed with powers of discretion, our hero declined. Meanwhile Isaac's heart was sore. The situation was galling. If there was to be no more fighting, why should he not get his release, join Wellington in Portugal, and renounce Canada? Unrest and vigilance best describe the order of his days, while waiting attack. The death of the ever-attentive Dobson, who had passed away before Brock's departure for Detroit, and the absence of the faithful sergeant-major—now Adjutant FitzGibbon—distressed him. In an attempt by General Brown to capture some British batteaux at Tousaint Island, on the St. Lawrence, the Americans had been repulsed by Brock's gallant protégé.

Everything now pointed to an early attack by the enemy in force. General Van Rensselaer, with an ascertained army of at least 6,300, of which 2,600 were militia, wrote that he " would cross the river in the rear of Fort George, take it by storm, carry the Heights of Queenston, destroy the British ships—the *Prince Regent* and *Earl Moira*—at the mouth of the river, leave Brock no rallying point, appal the minds of the Canadians, and wipe away the past disgrace."

On one of his visits to Fort George he had remarked to Brock, who had laughingly pointed out two beautiful brass howitzers taken from General Wayne, " Oh, yes, they are old friends of mine; I must take them back."

123

The Story of Isaac Brock

They were not taken back in Brock's time. Even with his grand army of 6,300, his 400 Seneca braves, and his written admission that Niagara was weakly garrisoned, it is certain Van Rensselaer would have still delayed attack, unless he had been told by his spies that Brock had returned to Detroit. Then, with valour oozing from his finger tips, he plucked up courage to attack the lair in the lion's absence.

At this juncture an untoward event occurred, in the re-taking by the Americans of the brig *Detroit,* formerly the United States brig *Adams*—captured, as we know, by Roulette—and the trading brig *Caledonia.* They were at anchor at the head of the Niagara River, off Black Rock. The irregular regiments of Hull's command, under the terms of surrender, were on board on their way to their Ohio homes, via Lake Erie and Buffalo. The two vessels reached Fort Erie harbour safely, and being rightly regarded by the British as immune from attack, were left undefended, in charge of an officer and nine men only, most of whom were voyageurs. In addition to the prisoners, the two brigs carried great quantities of fur and 600 packs of deer skins. During darkness Lieutenant Ellis, with three armed boats and 150 United States troops and sailors, dropped alongside. Roulette and his nine men fought desperately, one being killed and four wounded, but both vessels, of course, fell into the enemy's hands. This attack was contrary to the rules of war, and a violation of the sanctity of the flag which "continued to float as long as there were American prisoners on board, awaiting to be landed on United States soil."

"Hero, Defender, Saviour"

Brock regarded this loss as a calamity. It was, he wrote to Prevost, " likely to reduce him to great distress." His constant fears that the enemy would secure control of both Lakes Erie and Ontario were well founded. He begged Prevost to let him destroy the vessels Chauncey, the American, was building on Squaw Island. Prevost, of course, besought him to forbear. Isaac Brock, exasperated and with tied hands, was " doomed to the bitterest of all griefs, to see clearly and yet be able to do nothing." Yet while he worked in chains his preparedness was a source of wonder to those behind the scenes.

Even no less a critic than John Lovett, General Van Rensselaer's military secretary, was impressed with what he saw through his field-glasses from Lewiston heights. " Every three or four miles, on every eminence," he wrote a friend, " Brock has erected a snug battery, the last saucy argument of kings, poking their white noses and round black nostrils right upon your face, ready to spit fire and brimstone in your very teeth, if you were to offer to turn squatter on John Bull's land." Influenced by these signs of " business," the United States officers were ordered to " dress as much like their men as possible, so that at 150 yards they might not be recognized." This was probably due to one of the last orders issued by our hero, who warned his men that, when the enemy crossed the river, to withhold their musketry fire until he was well within range, and then, " if he lands, attack him at the point of the bayonet with determined resolution."

With clairvoyance that would have done credit to a mind-reader, Brock knew that attack was imminent. To him the wind that blew across the river October 12th was

The Story of Isaac Brock

laden with omens of war. The air seemed charged with the acrid smell of burnt powder. The muffled beat of drums, the smothered boom of artillery, the subdued clash of steel meeting steel, the stealthy tramp of armed men, seemed to encompass him.

.   .   .   .

Brock was at his headquarters. He gazed from the window. The storm outside was hurling great splashes of rain against the narrow casement. To and fro, over the carpeted floor, he paced that evening for an hour or more, uninterrupted and alone. It was thus he marshalled facts and weighed conclusions. Powerful brain and vigorous frame acted in concert. He was enjoying the fulfilment of the promise of his youth. God had been good. The world had been tolerant; his fellow-men—at least those who knew the real Isaac—loyally appreciative. The knowledge of his honours and fame stirred him to his soul. Not that he was any better, or abler, he meditated, than other men, but that when "opportunity" offered he was permitted to grasp it.

> " For every day I stand outside your door,
> And bid you wake and rise to fight and win."

The influence of the great truth as pronounced in the now familiar couplet inspired him. He recognized the source whence he derived whatever of success had followed his efforts, and prayed for greater sagacity, more vigour of body and tenacity of purpose, a complete surrender of self to the task before him; that if his life was

" Hero, Defender, Saviour "

to be the price of duty, he might place it on the altar of his country without one shred of compunction.

. . . .

He rang the bell for Porter—his body-servant since Dobson's death—directed him to see that the council room was lighted, that pens, ink, paper and cigars were in place, as a meeting of his staff was slated for nine, and sought his sanctum.

The Story of Isaac Brock

CHAPTER XXIV.

BROCK'S LAST COUNCIL.

It was long past midnight on the morning of Tuesday, October 13th, 1812, when Brock dismissed his advisory council of staff officers. An animated discussion had taken place over the strength of the enemy and the spot he might select to cross the river, for ruses had been resorted to by Van Rensselaer to deceive the British.

"I dare not, gentlemen," said our hero, in opening the debate, "weaken my flanks at Niagara and Erie, though I realize I am leaving Queenston not properly protected. I have just learned that General Dearborn states that while 'Tippecanoe' Harrison invades Canada, at Detroit, with 7,000 men—I do not think it necessary I should point out Detroit on the map," he added with a smile—"and while a United States squadron—not a British one, mark you—sweeps Lake Ontario from Sackett's Harbour, Dearborn himself will threaten Montreal from Lake Champlain. While the east and the west are thus being annexed by the enemy, our friend Van Rensselaer is to entertain us here.

"An ordinary boat, as we all know, can be rowed across the river at Queenston in less than ten minutes. Our spies have reported that forty batteaux, to carry forty men each, are in readiness at Tonawanda. Evans and Macdonell, when they called on Van Rensselaer, saw at least a dozen boats moored at Lewiston, some of which

POWDER MAGAZINE, FORT GEORGE, NIAGARA.

Built in 1796.

Brock's Last Council

could carry eighty men. During the deplorable armistice, as General Sheaffe is aware "—looking at that officer —" Van Rensselaer brought up 400 boats and batteaux from Ogdensburg and other points, all of his previously blockaded fleet, so the enemy has no lack of transport. The most effective disposition of our limited force is, I admit, somewhat of a problem. There is no use in evading the fact that in point of numbers and ordnance we are too weak, and as Sir George Prevost has written me not to expect any further aid, Colonel Talbot must send us a few of his militia."

"Macdonell," he said, turning to his aide, "will you write at once, to-night, to Colonel Talbot, at Port Talbot, stating that I am strongly induced to believe I will soon be attacked, and tell him that I wish him to send 200 men, the militia under his command, without delay, by water to Fort Erie."

This was Brock's last official letter dictated in council.

"General Sheaffe," he said, addressing that officer, "you, perhaps, know better than any of us the particulars of Van Rensselaer's appointment. It seems that he is an amateur soldier, pitchforked into command against his own will, a victim of New York State politics. While this is probably so, we must not run away with the idea that his other officers are no better, for, besides Generals Dearborn and Wadsworth—both soldiers of national repute—his cousin, Colonel Solomon Van Rensselaer, his chief of staff, is a first-class soldier, a proved fighting man. The latter is reported to be at the head of 750 well-trained militia, 300 of whom are selected soldiers, and fifty are said to know every inch of the river. Our

The Story of Isaac Brock

spies report the enemy could ferry 1,500 regulars across in seven trips.

" The safety of our redan on the Heights has given me some concern, but Dennis, Williams and others report that the height is inaccessible from the river side. If an attack in force is made at Queenston, we will have to concentrate every available man there—at the risk of weakening our flanks. Lewiston, as you have seen, is white with tents. At Fort Gray the enemy has two twenty-four-pounders, waiting to silence our eighteen-pounder in the redan. The Americans have several mortars and six-pounders on the river bank below Lewiston, ready to ship to any point by boats specially equipped, or to cover the landing of their troops on our side of the river, and to drive us back if we attempt to dispute their passage."

In district general orders prepared that night, the last official document signed by General Sir Isaac Brock, he directed, " in view of the imminence of hostilities, that no further communication be held with the enemy by flag of truce, or otherwise, unless by his special permission."

" I cannot allow looting," he said. " Arms and other property taken from the enemy are to be at all times reserved for the public service." Brock's example might have been followed to advantage in later Canadian campaigns. " I am calling," he continued, " a district court-martial for nine o'clock to-morrow morning, October 13th, for the trial of three prisoners, a captain and two subalterns of the 49th and 41st regiments."

That court-martial was not held.

On the day before, Major Evans and Colonel Macdonell had waited upon Van Rensselaer, with a letter from

Brock's Last Council

Brock proposing "an exchange of prisoners of war, to be returned immediately, on parole." The fact of no reply having been received to this, Brock regarded as ominous.

"I firmly believe, gentlemen," he proceeded, and his confidence and courage was infectious, "that I could at this moment, by a sudden dash, sweep everything before me between Fort Niagara and Buffalo, but our success would be transient. Disaffection and desertion is rife in the American camp. Only the other day we saw six poor fellows perish in mid-stream. To-day more deserters swam the river safely. Our own force, estimating even 200 Indians under Chief Brant and Captain Norton, though I expect less than 100 would be nearer the mark, cannot exceed 1,500 men of all arms. These units I have collected from Sandwich to Kingston. Many of our men, as no one knows better than Quartermaster Nichol, have received no pay, are wearing broken shoes—some have no shoes at all—no tents and little bedding. It is true that they bear the cold and wet with an admirable and truly happy content that excites my admiration, but it is no less a disgrace to the responsible authorities. Sir George Prevost, as you know, has told me 'not to expect any further aid'—the old parrot cry from headquarters, 'Not a man to spare.' Let me ask the chief of the Mohawks, who is present, how many warriors he can muster?"

John Brant, or *Thayendanegea,* as he was known among the Six Nation Indians, was the hereditary chief. At this time he was but a youth of eighteen—a graceful, dauntless stripling, of surprising activity, and well educated. At his side sat Captain Jacobs, a swarthy, stalwart brave,

The Story of Isaac Brock

famous for his immense strength, and Captain John Norton, an Englishman, and chief by adoption only, who, in consideration of Brant's youth, was acting as his deputy and spokesman. The latter said that since his return from Moraviantown, and the hunting season having commenced, many of his braves were absent, but he would pledge the Mohawks would muster, when wanted, over one hundred tried men. Thanking the chiefs for their assurances, Brock continued:

"The enemy has an army of over 6,000. The four twelve-pounders and two hundred muskets captured with the *Detroit* is a serious loss to us. If the *Detroit* is lost to us, however, she is of no further use to the enemy. We are, I repeat, greatly outweighted and outnumbered by the enemy, both in siege guns and artillery, and have no forge for heating shot. I have, as a matter of form, written this day to Sir George Prevost, restating my anxiety to increase our militia to 2,000 men, but pointing out the difficulties I shall encounter, and the fear that I shall not be able to effect my object with willing, well-disposed characters. Of one thing, gentlemen, I am convinced, that were it not for the number of Americans in our ranks we might defy all the efforts of the enemy against this part of the Province.

"As to 'forbearance,' which I am constantly urged by Sir George Prevost to adopt, you are entitled to my views. While forbearance may be productive of some good, I gravely doubt the wisdom of such a policy; but, let me add, I may not, perhaps, have the means of judging correctly. We cannot, however, disguise the fact we are standing alongside a loaded mine. Let us be prepared for the explosion. It may come at any moment. Vigilance, readiness and promptness must be our watchwords. Might I ask you to remember my family motto, ' He who guards never sleeps.' Even to-morrow may bring surprises—such stormy weather as we are having seems strangely suitable for covering an attack.

" I think, gentlemen, if we weigh well the character of our enemy, we shall find him disposed to brave the impediments of nature—when they afford him a probability of gaining his end by *surprise,* in preference to the certainty of meeting British troops *ready formed for his reception.* But do not, because we were successful at Detroit in stampeding the United States troops, cherish the impression that General Hull is a sample of American soldiery. If we *are* taken by surprise the attack will soon be known, for our range of beacons extends from the Sugar Loaf to Queenston, from Lundy's Lane to Pelham Heights. Signal guns, also, will announce any suspicious movement. One word in conclusion. As soldiers you know your duty, and I think you now all understand the position we are in—as far as I know it.

" General Sheaffe," he continued, turning to that officer, " I am much concerned as to the fate of this town, Niagara, if its namesake fort on the other side of the river should be tempted to forget the rules of war and bombard the private buildings here with hot-shot. However, we will do our best to give the invaders, when they do come, a warm reception. There are two things, Major," looking towards Evans, his brigade-major and intimate friend, " that our men must not omit to observe, namely, to

The Story of Isaac Brock

'trust God and keep their powder dry,' a most necessary precaution if these storms continue."

.   .   .   .

It is worthy of note that while Brock was in conference with his staff, expecting invasion any day, General Van Rensselaer, at Lewiston, was writing the subjoined brief historical despatch to his brigadier-general, Smythe:

"Sir,—To-night, October 12th, I shall attack the enemy's batteries on the Heights of Queenston."

.   .   .   .

The weather was tempestuous. Rain clouds shrouded the Heights of Queenston in a black pall. The wind romped and rioted in the foliage. Brock's estimate of the character of the enemy was a masterly one. Van Rensselaer was about to verify our hero's prediction.

BROCK'S MIDNIGHT GALLOP (Original painting by Charles W. Jefferys, O.S.A.)

The Midnight Gallop

CHAPTER XXV.

THE MIDNIGHT GALLOP.

WELL into the half-light of morning, long after the last of his staff, Evans, Glegg and Macdonell, had departed, Brock sat alone at his headquarters at Fort George, writing rapidly.

On the oak mantel, an antique clock chimed the passing of the historic hours, with deep, musical strokes.

Was it presentiment—a clearer understanding that comes to men of active brain and acute perception, during solitary vigil in the silence of night, when, with heart and soul stripped, they stand on the threshold of the great divide—that whispered to this "knight of the sword" his doom? Was it this clearer comprehension that caused our hero to bow his head as a faint message from an unseen messenger reached him? With a sigh of resignation he arose from the unfinished manuscript and passed on to his bedroom.

.   .   .   .

Boom! Boom! Boom!

.   .   .   .

A muffled, indistinct roar, a confusion of sounds, aroused the half-conscious sleeper. Brock sprang from his couch, partly dressed.

The antique clock chimed one—two—three!

"Listen," he muttered to himself, "that was not a

135

The Story of Isaac Brock

signal gun. Surely it was the sound of sustained firing."
As he unlocked the outer door, opening on the barrack-
square, the sky above faintly aglow with the light of warning beacons, the low, steady roll of musketry and louder
roar of distant cannon convinced him that this was far
more serious than "the war between sentries."

"My good Porter," he said, speaking calmly to his
excited servant, who, himself awakened, came rushing to
his master, "have Alfred saddled at once while I complete dressing, and inform Major Glegg and Colonel
Macdonell that I am off up the river to Queenston."

In another minute Isaac Brock was in the saddle.

As he passed through the gates, thrown open by the
sentry, a dragoon, mire from head to foot from furious
riding, handed him a despatch announcing that the enemy
had landed in force at Queenston. A second later, in
response to the pressure of his knees, his horse was carrying our hero at a wild gallop across the common that
separated his quarters from the upper village.

Day was near to breaking. The earth steamed from
the heavy rain. Passing objects rose out of the dark
mists, magnified and spectral.

At the residence of Captain John Powell, Brock reined
up. The household was astir, aroused by the ominous
roar of artillery carried down by the river from the gorge
above. He stayed, without dismounting, long enough to
take a cup of coffee brought to him by General Shaw's
daughter—a "stirrup cup"—his last. Then, giving his
charger the spur, he rode away to death and distinction,
tenderly waving a broken good-bye to the sad-eyed woman
at the porch. This was his betrothed, who faintly fluttered

136

The Midnight Gallop

her kerchief in weeping farewell to the gallant lover she would never see again.

Brushing his eyes and urging his big grey to greater speed, "Master Isaac," eager to reach the scene of trouble, struck across the village, his horse's hoof-beats bringing many a citizen to the door to "God speed him." Some came out to follow him, and many a good wife's face was pressed to the window to watch "The General! God bless and spare him," as he headed his charger for the Queenston Road and Brown's Point. Among the more zealous hastening after Brock were Judge Ralph Clench and a few old half-pay officers of His Majesty's service, who hurried to Queenston to range themselves in the ranks of the volunteers. Others joined as the signal guns and the bells of the church of St. Mark's and the court-house spread the alarm.

His road lay up hill. Seven miles back from the shore of Lake Ontario stretched the height of land, extending west from the river to the head of the lake—a gigantic natural dam, over 300 feet high and twenty miles through; a retaining wall of rock, the greatest original fresh-water *barrage* in the world.

He paused a moment at Frields to order the militia company there to follow. Close to Brown's Point he met another galloper, S. P. Jarvis, of the York volunteers, who was riding so furiously that he could not check his horse, but shouted as he flew by, "The Americans are crossing the river in force, sir." Jarvis wheeled and overtook the General, who, without reining up, slackened his speed sufficiently to tell the rider not to spare his horse, but to hurry on to Fort George and order General Sheaffe to bring up

The Story of Isaac Brock

his entire reserve and let loose Brant's Indian scouts. A mile or so farther on, Jarvis met Colonel Macdonell, in hot pursuit of their beloved commander. The aide, in his haste, had left his sword behind him, and borrowed a less modern sabre from Jarvis, who continued his mad gallop towards Fort George, little thinking he had seen the last of his gallant General and the dashing aide, meeting, a few minutes later, Major Glegg, also riding post haste to overtake the General.

Meanwhile our hero had halted for a moment at Brown's Point, only to learn that Cameron's Toronto company of volunteers had already started, on their own initiative, up the river. Riding hard, he overtook the excited militiamen. Speaking a word to the officer in charge, he wheeled his horse in the direction of the Heights, calling upon the detachment in his well-known voice, and in a way that never failed to exact obedience:

"Now, my men, follow me."

.   .   .   .

The east showed signs of approaching day, and Brock, only two miles from Queenston, was treated to a spectacle that quickened his pulses. Shells were bursting on the mountain side above the village. The shadows of the dying night were streaked with the light from an incessant fire of small-arms. Grapeshot and musket-balls were ploughing up inky river and grim highland. At Vrooman's battery, on Scott's Point, guarded by Heward's volunteer company from Little York, and some of Hatt's company of the 5th Lincoln militia, a mile from Queenston, the twenty-four-pound shells from the gun, mounted *en barbette,* which commanded at long range both landings,

The Midnight Gallop

were leaving behind them furrows of fire in the black gorge. The big gun was pouring a continuous stream of destructive metal upon the American boats that were attempting the passage of the river within the limited zone of its fire.*

Fort Gray, above Lewiston, was fairly belching flames, to which the isolated eighteen-pounder on the Queenston redan was roaring an angry and defiant response. Brock's trained ear recognized the wicked barking of the brass six-pounders, under Dennis of the 49th, mingling with the occasional boom of the twenty-four-pound carronade below the village.

The village of Queenston consisted of a small stone-barracks and twenty or more scattered dwellings in the midst of gardens and orchards. To Brock's right a road from the landing led to St. David's, from which, at almost right angles, an irregular branch roadway wound up the Heights. The adjacent table-land west of the village was dotted with farm-houses, partly surrounded by snake-fences and an occasional stone wall.

Above Vrooman's he was joined by his two aides. Here he met a few men, shockingly torn and bleeding, crawling to the houses for shelter, and quite a number of prisoners, and was told that the enemy was routed. All killed or taken prisoners! Very skeptical, but increasing his speed, our hero rode into the village, and, though stained and splashed with mud from stirrup to cockade, he was recognized, and welcomed by the men of the 49th with a ringing cheer.

*This gun is credited with having fired 160 shots during the engagement.

The Story of Isaac Brock

CHAPTER XXVI.

THE ATTACK ON THE REDAN.

CHECKING his reeking horse for a moment, Brock acknowledged with a smile the salute, saying to the men who had leaped to his side, " Take breath, my good fellows; you will need all you have, and more, in a few minutes," words which evoked much cheering. Then he breasted the rise at a canter, exposed to a galling enfilading fire of artillery, and running the gauntlet of the sniping of some invisible marksmen, reached the redan, half-way to the summit. Here he dismounted, threw his charger's reins to a gunner, and entered the enclosure.

.   .   .   .

From the loftier elevation of the Heights a still more striking scene confronted him. He saw, in the yellow light, battalion after battalion drawn up in rear of the Lewiston batteries, across the river, only two hundred yards wide at this point, awaiting embarkation. Other soldiers he saw crouching in the batteaux on the river, while an unknown number had already crossed and were in possession of Queenston landing. Round and grape shot from the American batteries were searching the banks and scourging the village, while shells from mortars at short range came singing across the river. He saw a boat with fifteen American soldiers smashed in mid-stream by a six-pounder from Dennis's battery, and watched the mangled bodies drift into the gloom.

.   .   .   .

BATTLE OF QUEENSTON HEIGHTS.

(From an old sketch credited to Captain Dennis.)

The Attack on the Redan

Having surveyed the position rapidly, ignorant of the concealed movements of the American troops, Brock at a first glance pronounced the situation favorable.

The crest of the Heights was wooded densely. The leaves still clung to the trees in all the spangled glory of autumn, and the thickets afforded far too safe cover for the American sharpshooters. In answer to his inquiry, Williams, in charge of the light company of the 49th, told him that at least 350 United States regulars and 250 militia must already have been ferried over. In the chilling gray of dawn, four boats, filled with armed men, had been seen crossing the river, which here had a four-mile current. The head of a column had also been seen above the river bank at the Queenston landing. The soldiers from the three batteaux, previously landed below Hamilton's garden, had already been met by Dennis's men, who had killed several and captured others. Later, more boats had come ashore, knocked out of commission by Vrooman's big gun and the six-pounders. Their crews had surrendered. Some of these Brock had met. Many more, however, had landed safely, hidden by the shadows, and were doubtless then awaiting a chance to emerge from ambush.

In answer to Brock's question as to whether there was a chance of the Height being scaled direct from the river, Williams repeated what he had already reported at the council meeting, that the scouts insisted that the Heights could not be climbed from the landing. The cliffs, over three hundred feet high, rose almost vertically from the water, and the denseness of the shrubs, tangle and over-hanging trees, anchored in the clefts, rendered it impos-

The Story of Isaac Brock

sible for any but exceptionally active and resolute men, and then only as a forlorn hope, to reach the summit. Projecting ledges of rock also blocked the way. A large body of men had been seen before daybreak stealing across the foot-hills, but had evaded pursuit. He believed they had fled to the Black Swamp, four miles distant.

Seeing that Dennis needed every possible support at the landing, Brock ordered Williams and his men to proceed to his assistance, and on the latter's departure our hero and his aides were left alone with the eight gunners.

.   .   .   .

The rain was gradually ceasing. Shafts of light from an unseen sun tinged the edges of the smoke-coloured clouds with amber and rose. A few spent musket-balls falling about the enclosure aroused Brock's suspicions. He was watching, from behind the earthen parapet, the flight of the shells discharged by the eighteen-pounder, and, seeing that they burst too soon, turned to the gunner.

" Sergeant, you are misjudging your time and distance; we must not waste powder and shot. Your shells are bursting too soon. Try a longer fuse."

The words were barely out of our hero's mouth when there was a rolling crash of musketry, accompanied by wild shouts, and a shower of bullets flew zipping over their heads. Shooting high is the invariable shortcoming of excited marksmen. A moment later the heads of a large force of American riflemen rose from the rocky ambuscade above and behind them. The next instant the enemy was in full charge, evidently bent on capturing both the General and the redan.

The Attack on the Redan

Brock saw that resistance would be madness. To save the gun and escape capture must be the "double event." Seizing a ramrod, he ordered an artilleryman to spike the gun, gave the command to retreat, telling the men to "duck their heads," fearing another discharge, and, leading his horse, followed by Macdonell and Glegg and the firing squad of eight artillerymen, rushed down the slope.

. . . .

For a clearer understanding of the situation—a better conception even than our hero had when, to escape capture and save the lives of his men, he was compelled to abandon the redan—we must visit Van Rensselaer's camp at Lewiston.

The Story of Isaac Brock

CHAPTER XXVII.

VAN RENSSELAER'S CAMP.

AFTER midnight, on the morning of the 11th, the American general, Van Rensselaer, believing, as he wrote, " that Brock, with all his disposable forces, had left for Detroit," launched from the Lewiston landing, under cover of the pitch darkness, thirteen boats capable of carrying 340 armed men.

To Lieutenant Sims, " the man of the greatest skill in the American service," was entrusted the command. Sims entered the leading boat, and vanished in the gloom. Whether he had taken all the oars with him, as reported, or whether the furious storm and the sight of the whirling black waters had frozen the hearts of the troops, must remain a mystery. The other boats did not follow.

Meanwhile, 350 additional regulars and thirty boats had arrived from Four Mile Creek. Flying artillery came from Fort Niagara, with still more regulars, and part of Smythe's brigade from Buffalo. Troops, as Brock's spies had truly reported, now overflowed the United States army headquarters—three more complete regiments from New York and another from Fort Schlosser. Lewiston bristled with bayonets. The entire expeditionary force was in command of Colonel Solomon Van Rensselaer, a militiaman, between whom and the officers commanding the regular troops much jealousy and great friction existed. Both branches of the service were determined

144

Van Rensselaer's Camp

to monopolize whatever credit might ensue. A storm, more furious than ever, prevailed for twenty-eight hours. The men sulked in their tents.

On the night of the 12th, the storm having abated, though the sky was black as ink, added numbers having developed greater courage, Van Rensselaer resolved on another attempt. He secretly notified Brigade-Major Smythe, in command at Buffalo, that in accordance with the letter reproduced in a previous chapter, he would storm the Heights of Queenston that night. With experienced river men as pilots, with picked crews, and protected by the big guns at Fort Gray, 600 men, with two pieces of light artillery, in thirteen boats, in the grim darkness of the morning of the 13th—a sinister coincidence—drew up in silence on the wharf. They comprised the first detachment of 850 regulars and 300 militia, the advance attacking party—"the flower of Wadsworth's army"—embarked to "carry the Heights of Queenston and appal the minds of Canadians."

Let us trace the fulfilling of Van Rensselaer's boast.

The regulars crossed first, almost out of the line of fire of the British batteries, and under cover of six of the enemy's field-guns that completely commanded the Canadian shore. Some of the boats of this flotilla effected, as we know, a landing above the rock, still visible at the water's edge, under the suspension bridge. Here they disembarked their fighting men—the 13th regulars and some artillery—and, under Van Rensselaer, attempted to form. The empty boats recrossed the river to ferry over more soldiers.

* * * * * * * * * *

The Story of Isaac Brock

A sentry of the 49th—our hero's regiment—overheard voices and tramping of feet. Scenting danger, he ran, without firing, to alarm the main guard.

In a few minutes Dennis advanced upon the landing place with forty-six men of his own company and a few militia, and discharged a murderous volley, leaving Colonel Van Rensselaer, with eight officers and forty-five men, killed or wounded. The enemy retreated to the water's edge for shelter, confused and shivering. The Lewiston batteries at once opened fire on the redan on Queenston Heights. The position of Dennis being thus revealed to Dearborn's gunners, they immediately turned their battery of six field-pieces upon his handful of men, and the position proving untenable, he withdrew to the shelter of the village, on the lip of the hill, still continuing to fire downwards on the invaders.

Vrooman's battery then opened fire, and Crowther brought his two "grasshoppers"—small three-pounders —to sweep the road leading to the river.

A Foreign Flag Flies on the Redan

CHAPTER XXVIII.

A FOREIGN FLAG FLIES ON THE REDAN.

IT was the crackling of the grenadiers' muskets, the bellowing of Vrooman's big gun, the cannonade of the twenty-four-pounders of the Lewiston batteries, the roar of the eighteen-pounder in the British redan, and the streak of crimson light from the long line of beacons which rent the sky from Fort Erie to Pelham Heights, that had wakened the citizens of Niagara and aroused Brock from his brief repose.

Captain Wool, of the 13th U. S. regulars—Van Rensselaer being wounded in six places—hurried his men under the shelter of the overhanging rocks, keeping up an intermittent fire, and waited for reinforcements. For almost two hours this desultory firing continued. With the cessation of the storm and arrival of broad daylight, six more boats attempted to reach the Queenston landing. One boat was sunk by a discharge of grape from Dennis's howitzer; another, with Colonel Fenwick, of the U. S. artillery, was swept below the landing to a cove where, in the attack by Cameron's volunteers that followed, Fenwick, terribly wounded, was, with most of his men, taken prisoner. Another boat drifted under Vrooman's, and was captured there, while others, more fortunate, landed two additional companies of the 13th, forty artillerymen and some militia. The shouts of the fighters and screams of the wounded were heard by the

The Story of Isaac Brock

hundreds of spectators who were parading the river bank at Lewiston, all ready to witness "the humiliation of Canada."

General Van Rensselaer had commanded that the "Heights had to be taken." Wool, a gallant soldier, only twenty-three, suffering from a bullet that had passed through both his thighs—no superior officer coming to his support—volunteered for the duty. He expressed his eagerness to make the attempt. Gansfort, a brother officer of Wool's, had been shown by a river guide a narrow, twisting trail, used at times by fishermen, leading to the summit. This he pointed out to Wool as a possible pathway to the Heights, where a force of determined men might gain the rear of the British position. Wool, at the same time, had also been informed that Williams, hitherto on the Heights, had been ordered to descend the hill to assist Dennis—which was Brock's first command on reaching the redan. Followed by Van Rensselaer's aide, who had orders "to shoot every man who faltered," Wool at once commenced the ascent, leaving one hundred of his men to protect the landing.

Picked artillerymen led the way. Concealed by rock and thicket, and unobserved by the British—the trail being regarded as impassable—they reached the hill-top, only thirty yards in rear of the solitary gun in the redan. The noise of their movements was drowned by the crash of the batteries, which reduced Hamilton's stone house to ruins and drove Crowther and his small gun out of range. The shells from the enemy's mortars rained upon the village, and his field-pieces subjected the gardens and orchards of Queenston to a searching inquisition.

A Foreign Flag Flies on the Redan

On reaching the summit, Wool, when the last straggler had arrived, formed his men, without losing a minute, and emerging from ambush, fired a badly-aimed volley at the astonished Brock and his eight gunners, and with a wild shout rushed down upon the redan.

. . . .

When the United States flag was raised over the gun, which Wool, to his deep chagrin, found spiked, the troops at Lewiston realized that the battery had been taken. Their courage returning, they rushed to the boats below, hoping to participate in a victory which, while hitherto a question in their minds, now seemed beyond all doubt.

Brock, on regaining the bottom of the slope, seeing that the main attack was to be made at Queenston, sent Captain Derenzy with a despatch to Sheaffe at Fort George.

" Instruct Major Evans," he wrote, " to turn every available gun on Fort Niagara, silence its batteries, and drive out the enemy, for I require every fighting man here; and if you have not already done so, forward the battalion companies of the 41st and the flank companies of militia, and join me without delay."

Mounting his horse, he galloped to the far end of the village. Here he held a hurried consultation with the few officers present, and despatched Macdonell to Vrooman's to bring up Heward's Little York volunteers at the double. He then instructed Glegg to order Dennis, with the light company of the 49th, less than fifty strong, and Chisholm's company of the York militia, to join him, and also to recall Williams and his detachment. When these arrived he took command.

The Story of Isaac Brock

"Captain Williams," said he, "how many men do you muster?"

"Seventy, sir, of all ranks," replied Williams; "forty-nine grenadiers and Captain Chisholm's company of volunteers."

"We must make the attempt, then," said the General, "to turn the enemy's left flank on the Heights, and this can only be done by a round-about way." Then, as Dennis joined him, he said, with a shade of vexation on his face, "It is a waste of time lamenting mistakes, but the over-looking of that pathway was a serious thing. The re-taking of the redan must be attempted at all hazards. It is the key, you see, to our position. If we wait for all our reinforcements the task will only be greater, as it will give the enemy time to establish himself in force, and when he drills out the spiked gun, the odds against us will be greater still."

Then, after a pause, "We must try and regain that gun without a moment's delay. It will be hot work, and means a sacrifice, but it is clearly our duty. Macdonell cannot be long. How are your men?"

"Somewhat fagged, sir," replied Dennis, "and a bit hippish. We've had a trying time, but they are ready to follow you."

.   .   .   .

It has been truly said of Isaac Brock that he never allowed a thought of self-preservation or self-interest to affect for one instant his conception of duty. He was blind at this moment to all personal considerations. He made no effort to shelter himself behind any plausible

150

A Foreign Flag Flies on the Redan

excuse that would have been gratefully seized by the timid or calculating man, or to fence with his duty. His consistency was sublime. "His last moments were in clear keeping with his life and his belief."

> "He who thinks in strife
> To earn a deathless fame,
> Must *do*, nor ever care for life."

The little band of heroes fell into line, while their brother hero addressed them.

"Men of the 49th," said Brock, "and my brave volunteers, I have heard of your work this morning, and the trying circumstances under which you have been fighting. Now, my lads, as you know, a large body of the enemy has stolen a march on us. They have taken our gun, it is true, but they will find it spiked! It is our duty to re-take it. Be prepared for slippery footing. Use every bit of shelter, but when we make the final rush give the enemy no time to think. Pour in a volley; fire low, and when it comes to in-fighting, use the bayonet resolutely and you have them beaten. I know I can depend upon you. . . . There is a foreign flag flying over a British gun. It must not stay there. . . . Don't cheer now, men, but save your breath and follow me."

.   .   .   .

There was a cheer, notwithstanding.

The Story of Isaac Brock

CHAPTER XXIX.

THE BATTLE OF QUEENSTON HEIGHTS.

WHILE these fateful and stirring scenes were being enacted at Queenston, a despatch rider arrived from Evans of Fort George. Without waiting for further instructions, he had, after Brock's departure, with the first glimpse of daylight, cannonaded Fort Niagara. This he did with typical thoroughness. His fire was returned with interest. With a license in direct opposition to the laws of battle, the enemy, under Captain Leonard, turned his guns on the village of Newark, bombarding public buildings and private residences with hot-shot, laying part of the town in ashes. This infuriated Evans, and he renewed the siege with so much vigour that he compelled the American garrison to evacuate. A shot from one of his twelve-pounders burst within the centre of Fort Niagara and decided Leonard to abandon his position in haste, after suffering many casualties.

.   .   .   .

Under a nasty crackle of musketry, galling and accurate, which harried the men, already chilled and strung up with suspense, the small detachment following the courageous Brock from the lower village soon reached the stone walls that surrounded a residence at the base of the hill. Here our hero dismounted, handed his horse to an orderly, and directed the men to find shelter. A moment later, taking advantage of a lull in the firing, he vaulted over the wall, and waving his sword above his head, shouted to the grenadiers a word of encouragement. They answered with a cheer, still following him as he led the way up the steep ascent towards the captured battery.

The Battle of Queenston Heights

Wool, within the enclosure of the redan, was closely watching the steady advance of the small body of resolute men breasting the Height.

The purpose of these men was unmistakable. As they drew closer, scarlet uniform and polished bayonet blazed and flashed in the sunshine. Having been heavily reinforced, he detached a party of 150 picked regulars, and with these moved out to meet the small band of British led by Brock. A brief exchange of shots took place, and the Americans fell back, firing.

Though the rain had ceased the trees were gemmed with drops that still dripped. The ground was strewn with wet leaves, slippery, and affording treacherous foothold. Progress was slow and laborious. As the hillside grew steeper, a man here and there slid, lurched and fell. To maintain any semblance of formation was impossible. The fire grew hotter. Ball and buckshot and half-ounce bullets down-poured on them from above. " Death crouched behind every rock and lurked in every hollow."

Had Brock's handful of loyalists been able to rush headlong, spurred by lust of conflict, and lock bayonets with the enemy, another tale might have been told. But the effect of the futile struggle for foothold on the hillside, seamed with slippery depressions, in the teeth of a blizzard of lead, soon showed. The bullet-swept ascent was a cruel test for men already fagged and faint. As for our hero, though storm-beaten, stained with mud, and hungry as a wolf, he was still the same indomitable youth who had scaled the cut cliffs of Cobo in search of seagulls' eggs. His vigour and disregard of danger were magnificent. His example, splendid.

The Story of Isaac Brock

Brock may not have been judicially precautious. Had he waited for reinforcements—there were none nearer than Fort George—his own life might possibly have been preserved. As an alternative he could perhaps have withdrawn and sought shelter in the village. But—apart from the peril to his own prestige—who would care to estimate the ulterior effect upon his men if such an example had been set them? These rough Canadian irregulars consisted, as they do to-day, of the finest fighting material in the world. The law of self-preservation had no place in the litany of Isaac Brock. He was a daily dealer in self-sacrifice. Besides, this was not the time or place to calculate involved issues. He was not a cold-blooded politician, nor was he an opportunist; he was merely a patriot and a soldier fighting for hearth and home, for flag and country. It was not an issue that could be left to arbitration in the hereafter, or threshed out by judge and jury. The situation called for instant action. To *do* his obvious duty rather than to *know* it, seemed to our hero the only honorable exit from the dilemma, even though it resulted in his own undoing.

Not until the dead are mustered by the God of hosts— at the last roll-call—will this noble soldier's conception of duty and his sacrifice be truly appraised.

God and the right was carved deep in the heart of Isaac Brock. Though he felt for his men, it was in a compassionate, not a weak way. War without bloodshed was inconceivable. He had been trained in an age and in a school that regarded blood-shedding in the protection of the right as wholly justifiable, as it was inevitable. Is there any change in respect to the application of this

The Battle of Queenston Heights

doctrine to-day? For himself he had no compassion whatever. His faith in the cause compelled him to fight to a finish. He was not of the potter's common clay of which fatalists are made. How many of these faithful fellows, he wondered, as his alert mind rapidly reviewed the present and recalled the past—Canadian and Celt, Irish and Anglo-Saxon, Protestant and Catholic, whom "neither politics, sect or creed could, in such a crisis, keep apart"—would leave their bodies to bleach on that hill-side? How many of them were destined to yield their lives for honour's sake, to die with their valour unrecorded in the defence—in the case of numbers of them —not of their own, but of their brother's rights?

.   .   .   .

The next second he was wondering what was doing at St. Peter's Port or London. It would be noon there. Were the good brothers and sister thinking of "Master Isaac" at that moment? Then, swifter than light, he was at Niagara, and the bowed figure of a woman at a porch, with pale, upturned face, who that morning had bade him a silent farewell, rose before him—surely it was years ago—the woman to whom he was betrothed. Then, in a flash, he turned to see some wavering figures around him, some of his own men—not a few wounded— who faltered and shrank from the screaming buckshot, and dropped to the rear.

The soldier awoke.

"This is the first time," he shouted, "I have ever seen the 49th turn their backs! Surely the heroes of Egmont will never tarnish their record!"

.   .   .   .

The rebuke stung. The panting ranks closed up.

155

The Story of Isaac Brock

CHAPTER XXX.

THE DEATH OF ISAAC BROCK.

AT this moment Colonel Macdonell, excited and eager to participate, reached the foot of the mountain at the head of the supports for which the General had despatched him. These consisted of about thirty of Heward's flank company of militia and thirty of the 49th—almost breathless and much exhausted, having run most of the way. Brock's small force—those actually at his side—were Chisholm's and Cameron's companies of the Toronto and York volunteers—a mere handful of perhaps eighty all told. These, together with Macdonell's men, who were at the foot of the hill on the right, now numbered less than 190 of all ranks.

For an instant there was a pause. Brock spoke hurriedly to his aide.

" If Williams and Macdonell can but outflank the Americans on the summit and scale the mountain in rear of the redan on the right, nothing can prevent our driving them out. Our place is here."

" But, General," interposed his aide, who worshipped his commanding officer, " I pray you, let me lead, or at least do take proper precautions. If you are wounded, think what may befall us."

" Master Glegg," hurriedly replied Brock, " I must remain at the head of these men. Duty and desire compel me. Should I fall, there are others not less competent."

DEATH OF ISAAC BROCK (Original painting by Charles W. Jefferys, O.S.A.)

The Death of Isaac Brock

A half smile, a touch of the arm, and the two men separated. A long separation.

. . . .

Deceived by the scarlet uniforms of the militia flank companies, Wool believed that the attacking party was composed exclusively of regulars, so steady was their advance. His own force now consisted of 500 men, over 300 of whom were regulars. Notwithstanding his much greater strength and vastly superior position, being protected by artificial brush-shelters and logs, and the withering fire with which he met the dogged progress of the British, his flanks, pressed by Williams and Macdonell, began to shrink. The moment was a critical one for our hero.

The supreme effort must be made.

Glancing below, Brock, even at that instant, for a fleeting moment was conscious of the beauty of the country spread beneath him. Almost as far as eye could reach extended an immense, partly pastoral plain, studded with villages, groves, winding streams, cultivated farms, orchards, vineyards and meadows. In places a dense forest, decorated with autumn's mellow tints, and furrowed by the black gorge of the Niagara, stretched to the horizon. Across all, shadows of racing clouds gave emphasis to the brilliant flood of sunshine. No fairer scene ever greeted the eye of man. The entire landscape breathed peace. Above it, however, in detached masses, hung lurid billows—the smoke of battle. . . . The serene vision faded, and in its place, in brutal contrast, came cruel, imperious bugle calls, the metallic rattle of fire-arms, the deep thunder of artillery, the curdling cry of wounded men.

Isaac's senses were insulted by the carnage of war.

. . . .

The Story of Isaac Brock

He now noticed that the supports, led by his plucky aide at the foot of the hill, were flagging. He shouted back, " Push on, York Volunteers !"

Our hero's robust figure was a conspicuous object for the American riflemen. While telling his men to take advantage of every bit of shelter, he paid little attention to himself. His uniform, his position at the head of his men, his loud words of command, stamped him a man of mark, a soldier of distinction, a special target for Wool's sharpshooters.

. . . .

So far he had escaped the hail of shot by a miracle. Picking his footsteps—it was treadmill work—he sprang forward, urging on his men by word and gesture.

. . . .

A deflected bullet struck the wrist of his sword arm. The wound was slight. He again waved his sword, smiling his indifference and still speaking words of encouragement.

. . . .

They were getting at close quarters now. The redan was less than fifty yards above.

He was calling to those nearest him to hold their fire a moment, to prepare to rush the enemy and use their bayonets, when, from a thorn thicket, an Ohio scout, Wilklow by name, one of Moseley's riflemen, stepped forward, and, singling out his victim, deliberately aimed at the General. Several of the 49th, noticing the man's movement, fired—but too late. The rifleman's bullet entered our hero's right breast, tore through his body on the left side, close to his heart, leaving a gaping wound.

. . . .

BROCK'S COAT WORN AT QUEENSTON HEIGHTS.

Showing hole made by entry of bullet.

The Death of Isaac Brock

Brock sank slowly to the ground, quite sensible of his grievous fate. A grenadier, horribly mutilated, fell across him. To those who ran to aid our hero, anxious to know the nature of his injury, he murmured a few broken sentences and—turned to die.

He tried to frame messages to loved ones, and then, more audibly, as he gallantly strove to raise his head to give emphasis to his last faltering words—the same Isaac Brock, unmindful of self and still mindful of duty—he said, "My fall must not be noticed, nor impede my brave companions from advancing to victory."

And with a sigh—expired.

.   .   .   .

Thus died General Sir Isaac Brock, defender and saviour of Upper Canada. Died the death he would have selected, the most splendid death of all—that of the hero in the hour of victory, fighting for King and country, for you and me, and with his face to the foe.

.   .   .   .

Our hero had passed his *last* milestone.

.   .   .   .

For a brief space the body of Isaac Brock rested where it had fallen, about one hundred yards west of the road that leads through Queenston, and a little eastward of an aged thorn bush.

.   .   .   .

Above the dead soldier's head, clouds, sunshine and rustling foliage; beneath it, fallen forest leaves, moist and fragrant. About the motionless body swayed tussocks

159

The Story of Isaac Brock

of tall grass and the trampled heads of wild-flowers. The shouts of the regulars, the clamor of the militia, the shrill war-cry of the Mohawks, and the organ notes of battle, were his requiem. Then the corpse was hurriedly borne by a few grief-stricken men of the 49th to a house in the village, occupied by Laura Secord—the future heroine of Lundy's Lane—where, concealed by blankets—owing to the presence of the enemy—it was allowed to remain for some hours, unvisited.

. . . .

Later in the day Major Glegg, Brock's faithful aide—the brave Macdonell, in extreme agony, lay dying of his wounds—hastened to the spot, and finding the body of his lamented friend undisturbed, conveyed it to Niagara, " where it was bedewed by weeping friends whose hearts were agonized with bitterest sorrow."

1 Queenston. 2 Field Piece. 3 Smoke, and the American Standard taken. 4 Niagara River. 5 Fort Grey Smoke A American B British ~

BATTLE OF QUEENSTON.

SUPPLEMENT

AFTER BROCK'S DEATH.

THE "Story of Isaac Brock" would be incomplete without an epitome of the events that terminated the Battle of Queenston Heights and resulted in an overwhelming victory for the British.

General Brock was killed in action at about half-past seven on the morning of October 13th, 1812. His body was removed from Government House, Niagara, to a cavalier bastion at Fort George, for final sepulture. This bastion was selected by Major Glegg, it being the one which Brock's own genius had lately suggested—the one from which the range of an observer's vision covered the principal points of approach—and had just been finished under his daily superintendence.

After he fell, the handful of men who were with him, overcome by his tragic end, overwhelmed by superior numbers and a hurricane of buckshot and bullets, wavered, and though Dennis attempted to rally them, fell back and retreated to the far end of Queenston village. Here, about two hours later, Colonel Macdonell, Brock's aide, collected and reformed the scattered units, and made another bold dash to rescale the heights and retake the redan. A detailed account of the incidents that followed in dramatic succession would fill a book.

With the cry of "Revenge the General!" from the men of the 49th, Macdonell, on Brock's charger, led the forlorn attack, supported by Dennis. At the same moment, Williams, with his detachment, emerged from the thicket, shouting to his men, "Feel firmly to the right, my lads; advance steadily, charge them home, and they cannot stand you." The two detachments then combined, and Macdonell ordering a general advance, they once more breasted the ascent.

The enemy, over four hundred strong, but without proper formation, fired an independent volley at the British as they approached to within thirty yards of the redoubt. This was

161

Supplement

responded to with vigour, and grenadiers and volunteers, in response to brave Macdonell's repeated calls, charged fiercely on Wool's men, now huddled in disorder around the eighteen-pounder. Some of them started to run towards the river bank. One American officer, Ogilvie, of the 13th regulars, thinking the situation hopeless, raised his handkerchief on his sword-point in token of surrender. Wool, a soldier of different calibre, tore it down, and a company of United States infantry coming at that moment to his assistance, he rallied his men.

The momentary advantage gained by Macdonell's small band of heroes was lost, and in the exchange of shots that followed, Macdonell's horse—Brock's charger—was killed under him, while he—his uniform torn with bullets—was thrown from the saddle as the animal plunged in its death struggle—receiving several ghastly bullet wounds, from which he died the following day, after enduring much agony. Williams, a moment later, fell desperately wounded; Dennis, suffering from a severe head wound, at first refused to quit the field, but Cameron having removed the sorely-stricken Macdonell, and Williams having recovered consciousness and escaped, the dispirited men fell back, retreated down the mountain at Parrott's Tavern, retiring upon Vrooman's battery. Here they awaited, unmolested, until two in the afternoon, the arrival of reinforcements from Fort George. The fight, though short, had been furious and deadly. Americans and British alike were glad to take breath.

Meanwhile, unobserved, young Brant, with 120 Mohawk Indians, had scaled the mountain, east of St. David's, outflanking the Americans, and hemmed them in until Captains Derenzy, of the 41st, and Holcroft, of the Artillery, arrived with the car-brigade from Fort George and trained two field-guns and a howitzer upon the landing. Merritt, with a troop of mounted infantry, at the same time reached the village by the Queenston road. This movement, which was a ruse, deceived the enemy, who at once redisposed his troops in readiness for an attack from this new quarter.

The American commander was ignorant of the fact that General Sheaffe—with four companies of the 41st, 308 strong, the same number of militia, and a company of negro troops from Niagara, refugee slaves from the United States—was at that moment approaching his rear in the rear of the Indians. The British

PLAN OF THE BATTLE OF QUEENSTON.

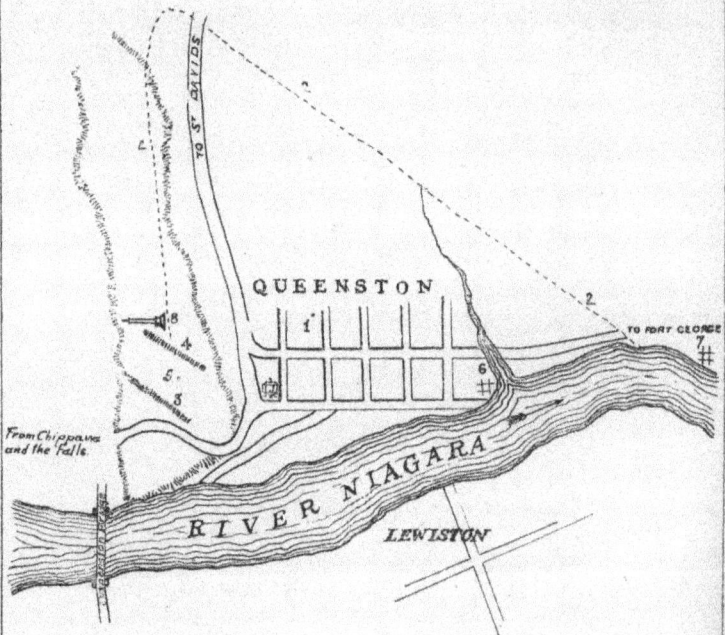

1. Spot where Brock fell.
2. { Road by which the reinforcements from Fort George gained the Heights in the afternoon.
3. American line as drawn up in afternoon.
4. British line   do   do.

5. Site of first monument
6. Old Fort
7. Vromont's Battery
8. Brock's monument.

(From an historical pamphlet).

Supplement

advanced in crescent-shaped formation, hidden by mountain and bush, and were shortly joined by a few more regulars and by two flank companies of the 2nd regiment of militia from Chippewa. Indeed, many persons of all ranks of life, even veterans exempt by age, seized their muskets and joined the column to repel the invaders, "unappalled" by Dearborn's threats of conquest or by the death of their "beloved hero, Isaac Brock." By this movement the British escaped the enfilading fire of the Lewiston batteries, the steep ascent of the heights in the teeth of the enemy's field-works, and compelled him to change front. The British of all ranks numbered less than one thousand.

The United States troops, which had been heavily reinforced, consisted at this time of about one thousand fighting men, on and about the mountain. This number was slowly supplemented by fresh arrivals from Lewiston, encouraged when they saw the American flag planted on the redan. The wounded were sent across the river. Nearly all of the new arrivals were regulars. Colonel Winfield Scott, of Mexican fame, a tried soldier, six feet four in his stockings, was now in command, supported by a second field-piece and many sharp-shooters. Van Rensselaer, narrowly escaping capture, had retreated by boat to Lewiston, ostensibly to bring over more troops. Finding the conditions unfavourable, he did not do so, but sent over General Wadsworth, as a vicarious sacrifice, to take command. The gun in the redan had been unspiked, and the summit strongly entrenched, but as Scott's men betrayed strange lukewarmness, orders were given "to shoot any man leaving his post."

Sheaffe's men having rested after their forced tramp, a few spherical case-shot by Holcroft drove out the American riflemen. His gunners had at last silenced the Lewiston batteries, and finding the river range, sunk almost every boat that attempted to cross. The Indians were now ordered to drive in the enemy's pickets slowly. Scouting the woods, they routed his outposts.

About four p.m. Captain Bullock, with two flank companies of militia and 150 men of the 41st, advanced, and after firing a volley in the face of a dense smoke, charged the enemy's right, which broke in great confusion. A general advance was ordered, and, with wild warwhoops by the Indians and white men, the

Supplement

heights were rushed, Wadsworth's veterans were stampeded, the redan retaken at the point of the bayonet, and Scott's command forced to the scarp of the cliff overhanging the river.

The American soldiers, to quote United States historians, now " fled like sheep," and scuttled off in all directions. Some raced headlong down the main road, seeking shelter under the muzzles of Holcroft's guns; some sought refuge in the houses; others raced to the landing only to find the boats no longer there. Not a few, hot pressed by Brant's avenging Mohawks, threw themselves over the precipice, preferring suicide to the redman's tomahawk. Others plunged into the Niagara, essaying to swim its irresistible eddies, only to be blown out of the green water by Holcroft's grapeshot or sucked down by the river's silent whirlpools.

One boat, with fifty struggling refugees, sank with its entire crew. Two others similarly laden were beached below the village, with only one dozen out of one hundred souls still living. The river presented a shocking scene. On the face of the water men, many maimed and wounded, fought and struggled for survival. This pitiful spectacle was actually taking place under the eyes of several thousands of American soldiers on the Lewiston bank, who, almost impossible to believe, and to their lasting disgrace, refused to join, or attempt even to succour, their comrades—deaf to all entreaty—allowing them to perish. Every room and shack at Queenston was an improvised hospital or morgue, filled with the mangled bodies of the quick and dead.

Cruikshank says 120 wounded United States officers and men were taken, of whom thirty died at hospital in Queenston and Niagara, while 140 more were ferried across to Lewiston. Lossing, the American historian, solemnly records the " fact " that " less than 600 American troops of all ranks ever landed at Queenston," and that " of these only 300 were overpowered "— some of the United States histories of the colonial wars need drastic revision—yet 958 American soldiers were taken prisoners by the British; " captured by a force," so officially wrote Colonel Van Rensselaer, after the battle, " amounting to only about *one-third* of the united number of the American troops." Captain Gist, of the U. S. army, placed their own killed at 400.

Among those who, when defeat was certain, fled to the water's edge, after fighting valiantly, was Colonel Winfield Scott, General

Supplement

Wadsworth, and other United States officers. Pursued by the Indians, they lowered themselves from shrub to shrub. When escape was hopeless, Scott tied the white cravat of his comrade, Totten, on his sword point, and with another officer, Gibson, was hurrying to present this flag of truce, when two Indians confronted them on the narrow trail. Jacobs, Brant's powerful follower, wrenched Scott's sword away, hatchets were drawn, and had not a British grenadier sergeant rushed forward, Winfield Scott would have fared badly.

General Van Rensselaer's defeat was complete and disastrous. His chagrin at his failure " to appal the minds of the Canadians " was so great that ten days later he resigned his command.

The account between Canada and the United States at sundown on that day stood as follows: Total American force engaged, 1,600. Killed and wounded, or sent back across the river, during the fight, 500. Prisoners, 73 officers, including two generals and five colonels, together with 852 rank and file. Total loss, 1,425 men, besides the colours of the New York regiment, one six-pounder, 815 carbines and bayonets, and 5,950 rounds of ball and buckshot.

The total British force engaged was 1,000. Of these 800 were regulars and militia, and 200 Indians. Killed, 14, including one major-general and one aide. Wounded and missing, 96. Total American loss, 1,425. Total British loss, 110. *The next day the British General, Sheaffe, Isaac Brock's successor, signed another armistice. The second armistice within a period of nine weeks!*

Such is the story of the Battle of Queenston Heights.

SUBSEQUENT EVENTS OF THE CAMPAIGN OF 1812.

AFTER Van Rensselaer resigned his command in favour of Brigadier-General Smyth, the effect of the British victory upon the United States troops at Lewiston was beyond belief. While the British soldiers were, with characteristic indifference, hard at work at Fort George cutting wood and threshing straw, the American soldiers across the river, according to their own historians, were deserting by the hundreds. Of General Tannehill's brigade of 1,414 of all ranks, 1,147 deserted within a few days. Twenty of these were officers.

Had the British been allowed to profit by this demoralization

Supplement

of the enemy and followed up their brilliant successes, they could, as Brock predicted, have swept the frontier from Chippewa to Sackett's Harbour, and probably prevented a continuance of the two years' war. The Sheaffe-Prevost inexcusable thirty days' truce was the very respite the enemy had prayed for. More men and more munitions were hurriedly despatched to all the United States frontier forts, and renewed courage imparted to some of the commanders and their hesitating brigades. The first to waken up after the expiration of this, to the Americans, merciful truce, was General Dearborn, who, with 2,000 men, attacked Odelltown, only to be driven back to Lake Champlain by de Salaberry. This reverse was followed in the last days of November by an attack by General Smyth, with 400 of his 4,300 men, upon a four-gun battery, defended by sixty-five men, above Garden Island, on the Niagara River. Elated with his success, he took for his rallying cry, "The cannon lost at Detroit—or death!" and again crossed the river with thirty-two boats and 900 men, and descended upon Fort Erie. Meanwhile, Colonel Bisshopp had retaken the fort, with its American captors, and with a handful of regulars and militia awaited "annihilation." As Smyth's flotilla advanced, Bisshopp poured in a hot fire, sinking two boats. This reception did not accord with Smyth's views of the ethics of war, and forgetting all about the "lost guns," and disliking, upon reflection, the idea of "death," he at once turned tail. At Buffalo he was publicly pelted by the populace, and for his cowardice was dismissed the service by the United States Senate without the formality of a trial. Dearborn—strange to say—having for the time lost his taste for fighting, went into winter quarters, and Canada, in universal mourning for Brock, but still confident and undaunted, rested on her arms. The year 1812 closed without further incident.

The period thus ended had been a momentous one. Brilliant reputations had been made and lost. The blood of many patriots had flowed freely, but, as regarded Canada, not in vain, for, in the words of the American historian, Schouler, "the war had impressed upon the people of the Republic the fact that Canada could not be carried by dash, nor pierced by an army officered by political generals and the invincibles of peace."

Supplement

THE CAMPAIGN OF 1813.

Though it would be quite natural to suppose that the story of Isaac Brock would end with his death and the victory of Queenston Heights, it is well to remember that the *influence of his triumphs only ceased with the close of the war* and the Treaty of Ghent, in December, 1814. Hence a *résumé* of the events that occurred during 1813 and 1814 is necessary, if a just valuation of our hero's achievements is desired.

Between July, 1812 and November 5th, 1814, " twelve distinct invasions of Canada by superior forces of the enemy were defeated." Out of fifty-six military and naval engagements between the British and U. S. forces, thirty-six were won by the British. Though the victories of 1812 were the direct factors that brought about a change in the national destiny of Canada, " Queenston Heights was not the culminating feat of arms." As a result of brooding over these disasters that had befallen the " Grand Army of the West," and the " national disgrace " of overwhelming defeat, the people of the United States, as a whole, independent of politics, " were now "—so write American chroniclers—" compelled to become belligerents."

In consequence of this national thirst for revenge, Generals Harrison and Winchester started to look for trouble in January, 1813, and—were rewarded. Strongly stockaded at Frenchtown, on the Ráisin River, with a seasoned army, they invited attack. Colonel Procter, with 500 soldiers and 800 Indians under Roundhead, accepted the challenge, and making a furious attack upon Winchester before daybreak, took the General and 405 of his " Grand Army " prisoners. Brockville was then raided, and fifty-two citizens kidnapped by the U. S. soldiers. During the next two years raids of this nature were of frequent occurrence, first by one belligerent, then by the other, and with varying success. Major Macdonald's capture of Ogdensburg, when he took eleven guns and 500 U. S. soldiers, was the next big win for Canada.

In April, to balance the account, General Pike descended upon York. The capital of Upper Canada at that time had a population of only 1,000, and was weakly garrisoned. While the enemy was advancing upon the small fort to the west of the village, a powder magazine exploded, killing many on

Supplement

both sides. General Sheaffe, thoroughly alarmed at the prospect, destroyed his stores, and, after 300 of his force had been captured, retreated with the remainder to Kingston—for which he was severely censured—and York surrendered. Then Procter, inflated by his victory at Frenchtown, and overrating his military skill, attacked Fort Meigs, on the Maumee River, was badly repulsed, and hopelessly lost all prestige.

This defeat of the British was followed by Dearborn's assault upon Fort George. With 7,000 men behind him, aided by the guns of Chauncey's fleet at the river mouth, he captured the time-worn fortification, and the Niagara frontier—despite the dogged resistance of General Vincent, who had to retreat with the crippled remnant of his 1,400 men—was at last in the possession of the enemy. This win was made more complete by General Prevost's belated and, of course, futile attack upon Sackett's Harbour. When assured success stared him in the face, his flaccid nature suggested retreat, and what might have been a signal victory became a disgraceful failure. The position of affairs at this time was admirably summed up in a letter written by Quartermaster Nichol. "Alas! we are no longer commanded by Isaac Brock. . . . Confidence seems to have vanished from the land, and gloomy despondency in those who are at our head has taken its place." Brock's courage, judgment, military skill and personal magnetism were never so much needed.

To offset these reverses, the brilliant victory of the British ship *Shannon* over the American war vessel *Chesapeake*, in a naval duel fought outside Boston harbour, somewhat restored British complacence. This was the prelude to another victory on land. Vincent, after being bombarded out of Fort George, slowly retreated with his broken command towards Burlington, cleverly flirting with the enemy, and drawing him farther and farther inland, finally reforming his wearied men near Stony Creek, sixteen miles from the lake's head. Here the enemy, 3,000 strong, went into camp. It was here that FitzGibbon— General Brock's old-time sergeant-major and faithful *protégé*— now in command of a company of the 49th, disguised as a settler, penetrated the enemy's camp, and was convinced a night attack would be successful. While the advance guard of the enemy was driving in the British decoy pickets, 800 of Vincent's force,

Supplement

under Harvey, surprised and charged them in the darkness, capturing two American generals, 120 prisoners, and four cannon, without the loss of a man.

Sheaffe was now transferred to Montreal, and De Rottenberg assumed military command in Upper Canada. Three weeks later an American, Colonel Boerstler, was ordered to surprise a small party of British at Beaver Dams (now Thorold). Lieutenant FitzGibbon, in command, was informed of the proposed attack. An heroic woman—Laura Secord—the wife of a wounded militiaman at Queenston, and to whose house Brock's body was borne after he fell, learned of the pending surprise by overhearing a conversation between some American officers. Her resolution was soon formed. Despite the fact that twenty miles through gloomy forest, filled with hostile Indians, lay between her home and the British camp, she tramped the distance unattended, though not unmolested, and reached the Stone House in time to warn the plucky grenadier. The wily Irishman at once despatched a party of Caughnawaga Indians to divert the enemy's attention. Advancing with a few soldiers, and finding Boerstler and his force drawn up in an opening of the woods, uncertain what to do, he boldly ordered that officer to surrender with his entire command of 540 soldiers, though he had but forty-seven men to enforce the conditions. His demand was instantly complied with.

To equalize in part this game of international see-saw, Chauncey again visited York with fourteen ships, mounting 114 guns, and plundered the defenceless capital.

On Lake Erie, Perry, with nine ships and a total broadside of 936 pounds of metal, defeated Barclay's six Canadian ships, with a total broadside of 459 pounds. These facts must be taken into impartial consideration in weighing the issue. In the west, Procter, still suffering from the shock received at Fort Meigs, with 407 troops and 800 Indians, retreated up the Thames valley, neglecting to burn his bridges in his retreat, with General Harrison and an army of 3,500 men in hot pursuit. The American general brought him to bay at Moraviantown, and in the frozen swamps the dispirited British, having lost all confidence in their fleeing commander, surrendered or escaped. It was here that the gallant and high-minded Tecumseh met his death, under distressing circumstances. The story was circulated that, mortified at Procter's proposed flight, the Shawanese chief was

169

Supplement

only restrained from shooting that officer by the interference of Colonel Elliott. For his conduct and the unexplained disaster at Moraviantown, Procter was court-martialed, severely condemned, and suspended from his command for six months.

The defeat of Procter was counterbalanced, however, by Colonel de Salaberry's dramatic victory over General Hampton. With 350 French Canadian Voltigeurs he hypnotized 3,500 United States troops at Chateauguay. When the fight was hottest the gallant Frenchman ordered his buglers to sound the advance, an alarming fanfare, accompanied by discharges of musketry from various points of the surrounding forest, and the enemy, thinking he was about to be attacked and flanked by superior numbers, was seized with panic, stampeded, and never halted in his retreat until he had placed twenty-five miles of country between him and the "French devils." After this, occurred the historic battle of Chrysler's Farm, on the St. Lawrence, when 2,000 U. S. regulars under General Boyd, with six field-guns, were routed, with a loss of 102 killed and 237 wounded, by a force composed of 380 regulars, militia and Indians, under Colonel Morrison, and driven back into American territory.

In the second week of December, General McClure evacuated Fort George, but before doing so burned 149 of the public buildings and private houses in Newark and Queenston, by order of John Armstrong, U. S. Secretary of War, compelling 400 women and children to seek shelter in the woods, with the thermometer ranging around zero. Even Lossing, the American historian, condemned this as "a wanton act, contrary to the usages of war, and leaving a stain upon the American character." The outrage brought its own punishment within the week. Colonel Murray, with 550 soldiers, captured the United States Fort Niagara, killing sixty-five men and taking 344 prisoners, and before the close of the year, with his heart on fire, the British general, Riall, crossed the river with 500 Indians and sacked Lewiston, Youngstown, Tuscarora and Manchester, only desisting from his excusable incendiarism when he had burned Buffalo and laid Black Rock in ashes. January 1st, 1814, was ushered in with the Cross of St. George floating over the battered ramparts of the American Fort Niagara.

Thus ended the year of our Lord 1813, for ever memorable in North American history as a twelve months of almost inces-

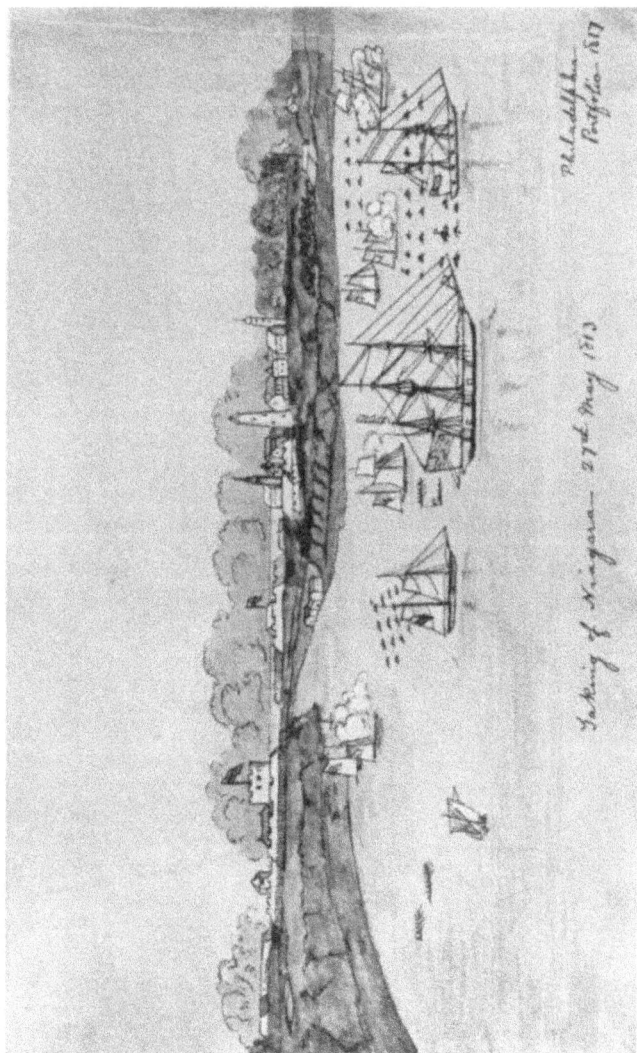

Taking of Niagara 27ᵗʰ May 1813

Philadelphia
Portfolio 817

TAKING OF NIAGARA, 27TH MAY, 1813.

(From print in Philadelphia "Portfolio," 1817.)

Supplement

sant warfare, famous for its records of conspicuous courage, much military incompetence, and great and lamentable carnage. A year, notwithstanding its sheaf of blunders, that should be canonized by all true Canadians, for it was a year that emphasized in an astounding manner the pluck and bull-dog tenacity of the Canadian militiaman, disclosing his deep love for country that resisted unto death the lawless attacks of a wanton invader.

THE CAMPAIGN OF 1814.

In March, 1814, General Wilkinson again undertook the forlorn hope of capturing Canada, leading 5,000 men against 350 British, under Hancock, at Lacolle, on Lake Champlain. After five hours of red-hot fighting, he was compelled to fall back on Plattsburg. A month later Admiral Sir James Yeo and General Drummond, with 750 men, landed under the batteries at Oswego, and in the teeth of a sustained fire of cannon and musketry, " gathered in " that historic town and sixty prisoners.

To and fro, like a pendulum, swayed the scene of action—to-day east, to-morrow west. Colonel Campbell and 500 American soldiers, with nothing better to do, made a bonfire of Port Dover, the incident being officially described by the U. S. War Department as " an error of judgment." Then General Brown, backed by an army of 6,000 U. S. veterans, swooped down like " a wolf on the fold " on Fort George, and annexed it and the garrison of 170 men. The British general, Riall, still possessing the fighting mania, and some 1,800 men, locked horns with General Brown and 3,000 of his veterans, and the Battle of Chippewa added another victory to the American record. The enemy then pillaged St. David's, while Riall—both sides having suffered heavily —retreated to the head of Lundy's Lane, a narrow roadway close to the Falls of Niagara, and stood at bay.

Three weeks elapsed, when General Drummond, realizing Riall's danger, hastened from York to his assistance, reaching Lundy's Lane with 800 men at the moment that General Brown, with his reinforced army of over 4,000 men, was within 600 yards of the British outposts. A moment later the contest was on, the bloodiest and probably the most brilliant battle of the whole campaign. It was a bitterly contested fight for seven hours—a death struggle for the survival of the fittest. During the first

171

Supplement

three hours the British force numbered only 1,640, until reinforced by 1,200 additional combatants. All through the long hours of the black night the battle waged furiously. Charge succeeded charge, followed by the screams of the mutilated and the dead silence of the stricken. Over all boomed the muffled thunders of Niagara. The big guns, almost mouth to mouth, roared crimson destruction. Though bayonets were crossed, and the fighting was hand to hand and desperate, and sand and grass grew ghastly and slippery with the sheen of blood in the fitful moonlight, the British, notwithstanding the advantage in weight and numbers of the enemy, held their ground. When day was breaking, and the American general found his casualties exceeded one thousand, he withdrew his shattered army of invaders to Fort Erie. The British loss was 84 killed and 557 wounded. Lundy's Lane has been likened to the storming of St. Sebastian or the deathly duel at Quatre Bras. Both invaders and defenders exhibited heroism—worthy, in the case of the enemy, of a higher cause. General Drummond was wounded, and a son of General Hull, of Detroit notoriety, was among the killed.

Though the battle of Lundy's Lane, fought on July 25th, was the last great engagement in 1814, and practically ended the war, the campaign was not destined to close without an exhibition of constitutional timidity on the part of Prevost, the man with the liquid backbone. With 11,000 seasoned veterans who had campaigned under Wellington, he advanced, September 14th, on Plattsburg, garrisoned by only 4,000 Americans, and when victory smiled in his face, he actually ordered the retreat. Overcome with humiliation, his officers broke their swords, declaring they "could never serve again," and sullenly retraced their steps to the frontier. This was the crowning episode that destroyed Prevost's reputation. Death rescued him from the disgrace of court-martial.

How clear-cut and free from blemish, in contrast with that of many of his contemporaries, stands out the brilliant record of Isaac Brock.

The Treaty of Ghent—while satisfactory to the people of Canada, bringing as it did a cessation of hostilities, permanent peace, and recognition of their rights—was received with mixed satisfaction by both political parties in the United States, after the first flush of excitement had passed away. "What," the

CENOTAPH, QUEENSTON HEIGHTS.

Erected near the spot where Brock fell.

Supplement

citizens asked each other, " have we gained by a war into which the country was dragged by President Madison in defence of free-trade and sailors' rights, and in opposition to paper blockades?"

In the articles of peace, these vexed questions (as related in Chapters VIII. and XIV.)—questions which, as we have seen, were advanced by the United States Government as the *real cause for war*, were *not even mentioned.* Some worthy Americans, having suffered from the fighting qualities of the Canadian loyalists, publicly stated that the " declaration of peace had delivered them from great peril." In some of the States " the universal joy was so great," writes Gay, in his Life of Madison, " that Republicans and Democrats forgot their differences and hates and wept and laughed by turns in each others' arms, and kissed each other like women."

Another United States historian (Johnston) writes that " peace secured not *one* of the objects for which war had been declared, for, though Britain put a stop to the irritating . . . practice of searching American vessels flying an American flag, she was not bound by the terms of the treaty to do so." In the words of another recorder (Taylor), " Britain ceased the practice of search, not on account of war, nor of the treaty, but because the necessity of doing so had passed away—the European war being over."

WHAT OF CANADA?

Canada, young as she was in the arts of peace and cruel practices of war, while honouring the memory of her heroes who had fallen in the splendid struggle against invasion, wasted no time in idle tears. The very atmosphere of her high northern latitude, the breath of life that rose from lake and forest, prairie and mountain, was fast developing a race of men with bodies enduring as iron and minds as highly tempered as steel. She drew another and a deeper breath, and, forecasting her destiny, with shoulders squared and fixed resolve, made ready to create an empire of industrial greatness which, under Providence, was to rank second to none.

The influence of Brock's life, achievements and death upon the Canadian people was more far-reaching than boy, or even man, would suppose. It aroused in the people not only the

173

Supplement

questionable human desire to avenge his death, but an unex-
pressed resolve to emulate his high manliness, his fixity of purpose, and his well-ordered courage in defence of the right.

. . . .

It remains for the youth of Canada to proudly cherish the
memory of Isaac Brock, and to never lose an opportunity to
follow the example he set for them by his splendid deeds.

BROCK'S MONUMENT.

Erected 1853.

APPENDIX.

EXPLANATORY NOTES ON THE ILLUSTRATIONS.

No. 1. FRONTISPIECE.

Major-General Sir Isaac Brock.

Reproduction of a copy of the original water-color and chalk drawing in the possession of Sir Isaac Brock's great-niece, Miss Tupper, of Candee, Guernsey. Copied for Miss Agnes FitzGibbon, of Toronto, by Alyn Williams, President of the Miniature Painters' Association of Great Britain, 1897, and not hitherto published. Adjudged by relatives to be an exact facsimile of Williams' portrait. Miss FitzGibbon writes that " the original painting is on similar paper to that on which Major-General Brock's last general orders are written, the size corresponding to the space between the watermarks. Dated 1811." Artist unknown.

No. 2. FACING PAGE 11.

" St. Peter's Port, Guernsey, in 18 × 6."

By an unknown artist. (An × was frequently used for a " 0 " at that time.) The original drawing was found among a number of unframed prints in a collection obtained by John Naegely, Esq., who presented it to the Grange Club, Guernsey, in 1870. It now hangs over the mantelpiece in the club reception room. The original is drawn in very fine pencil and water-color—a style of art fashionable at that period. Photographed for Miss Agnes Fitz-Gibbon in 1902. Brock's father's house, where our hero was born —now converted into a wholesale merchant's warehouse—stands at the point where two lines, drawn from the spots indicated by a cross (+) on the margin, would intersect. On the frame above the picture are the words, *" Guernsey in 18 × 6 ";* below, *" Pre-sented to the Grange Club by John Naegely, Esq., 9th March, 1870."*

Appendix

Appendix

Persons interested in military matters will observe that the white ostrich plumes, which show very slightly, are placed under the flaps, only the white edges appearing. This new style of feather display was, it is stated, in compliance with an order from the War Office, issued shortly before Brock's death. Previously the plumes were worn more conspicuously.

No. 8. FACING PAGE 75.

Butler's Barracks (Officers' Quarters), Niagara Common.

View of officers' quarters. From photograph loaned by Miss Carnochan.

No. 9. FACING PAGE 96.

Our Hero meets Tecumseh. "This is a man!"

Original black and white drawing by Fergus Kyle, Toronto. See page 97.

No. 10. FACING PAGE 109.

Lieut.-Colonel John Macdonell.

Reproduced, by permission, from A. C. Casselman's "Richardson's War of 1812." From a silhouette in possession of John Alexander Macdonell, K.C., Alexandria, Ontario. Colonel Macdonell, who was provincial aide-de-camp to Brock, was member of Parliament for Glengarry and Attorney-General of Upper Canada. Died, October 14th, 1812, from wounds received at battle of Queenston Heights, aged 27.

No. 11. FACING PAGE 117.

Queenston Heights and Brock's Monument.

As it appeared about 1830, excepting that the present monument has been substituted for the old one. Original water-color painting by C. M. Manly, A.R.C.A., Toronto, from a photograph in possession of Miss Carnochan.

Appendix

No. 12. FACING PAGE 121.

"Major-General Brock, 18 × 6."

From a vignette photograph loaned by Miss FitzGibbon, Toronto, and now published for the first time in any Life of Brock. As doubt has been expressed by some admirers of Brock as to the authenticity of this portrait, Miss FitzGibbon's written endorsation is here quoted:

"The photograph is from an original miniature portrait of Major-General (afterwards Sir) Isaac Brock, painted by J. Hudson, 18 × 6—1806—the date of General Brock's last visit to England. The miniature is now in possession of Miss S. Mickle, Toronto."

This full-face vignette is of exceptional interest, all other portraits of Brock being in profile, and is likely to challenge preconceived notions.

No. 13. FACING PAGE 128.

Powder Magazine, Fort George, Niagara.

This powder magazine was first built in 1796. Reproduced from a photograph in possession of Miss Carnochan, Niagara.

No. 14. FACING PAGE 135.

Brock's Midnight Gallop.

Original water-color painting by Charles W. Jefferys, O.S.A., Toronto. As a matter of fact, the hour of Brock's gallop from Fort George to Queenston, as described in Chapter XXV., was not "midnight," but shortly before daybreak. It is this time, "between the lights," with sky and atmosphere aglow from the fire of the batteries, that the artist cleverly depicts.

No. 15. FACING PAGE 140.

Battle of Queenston Heights.

Photographed in Guernsey, 1902, from a curious old print, from a sketch by a brother officer of Brock's—presumably Dennis. (See Explanatory Note to No. 18.) Loaned by Miss FitzGibbon. Original in possession of Miss Helen Tupper, Guernsey.

Appendix

No. 16. FACING PAGE 156.

Death of Isaac Brock.

Original water-color sketch by Charles W. Jefferys, O.S.A., Toronto. Shows our hero falling after being hit by the fatal bullet fired by an Ohio rifleman, while courageously heading the charge in the attempt to recapture the redan.

No. 17. FACING PAGE 159.

Brock's Coat, worn at Queenston Heights.

From photograph, loaned by Miss FitzGibbon, of the coat worn by Brock at Queenston Heights, showing the hole made by the entry of the fatal bullet. Photographed, 1902, from the original in the possession of Miss Tupper, of Guernsey.

No. 18. FACING PAGE 161.

Battle of Queenston.

Facsimile drawing by Harry Carter, Toronto, of an old sketch credited to Major Dennis (page 161), which appears on an early map of Upper Canada, published by O. G. Steele—presumably of Buffalo—in 1840. Underneath the original print are the following words, reproduced *verbatim:*

" BATTLE OF QUEENSTON.
AFTER A SKETCH BY MAJOR DENNIS,
13TH OCT., 1813,

Which ended in a complete victory on the part of the British, having captured 927 men, killed or wounded about 500, taken 1,400 stand of arms, a six-pounder, and a stand of colors."

(See, also, Explanatory Note to No. 15.)

No. 19. FACING PAGE 163.

Plan of Battle of Queenston.

Reproduced from an historical pamphlet loaned by Mrs. Currie, of Niagara, showing the plan of battleground, disposition of troops, and topography of adjacent country.

Appendix

No. 20. Facing Page 170.

Taking of Niagara, May 27th, 1813.

From a sketch which appeared in the Philadelphia *Portfolio*, 1817. Interesting from the fact that it is the only picture known which shows the churches of St. Mark's and St. Andrew's, Niagara (Newark), Canadian side, and the lighthouse which, built in 1803, stood on the spot where Fort Mississauga now stands.

No. 21. Facing Page 172.

Cenotaph, Queenston Heights.

Erected near the spot where Brock fell. It bears the following inscription:

" Near this Spot
Major-General
Sir Isaac Brock, K.C.B.,
Provisional Lieutenant-Governor of
Upper Canada,
Fell on 13th October, 1812,
While advancing to repel the
invading Enemy."

No. 22. Facing Page 174.

Brock's Monument.

On October 13th, 1824, the remains of Brock and his gallant aide, Macdonell, were removed from the bastion at Fort George and placed in a vault beneath the monument which had been erected on Queenston Heights by the Legislature to commemorate our hero's death. On Good Friday, April 17th, 1840, this monument was shattered by an explosion of gunpowder placed within the basement by a rebel of 1837 named Lett. In 1853 the corner-stone of a new monument, as shown at page 174, the cost of which was borne by the people of Canada, was erected on the same spot, and on October 13th, forty-one years after the British victory at Queenston, and the anniversary of Brock's splendid death, the remains of the two heroes were re-interred and deposited in two massive stone sarcophagi in the vault of the

Appendix

new monument. On the two oval silver plates on Brock's coffin was inscribed the following epitaph:

" HERE LIE THE EARTHLY REMAINS OF A BRAVE
AND VIRTUOUS HERO,
MAJOR-GENERAL SIR ISAAC BROCK,
COMMANDER OF THE BRITISH FORCES,
AND PRESIDENT ADMINISTERING
THE GOVERNMENT OF UPPER CANADA,
WHO FELL WHEN GLORIOUSLY ENGAGING THE ENEMIES
OF HIS COUNTRY,
AT THE HEAD OF THE FLANK COMPANIES
OF THE 49TH REGIMENT,
IN THE TOWN OF QUEENSTON,
ON THE MORNING OF THE 13TH OCTOBER, 1812,
AGED 42 YEARS.

J. B. GLEGG, A.D.C."

INDEX

www.ingramcontent.com/pod-product-compliance
Lightning Source LLC
Chambersburg PA
CBHW032048080426
42733CB00006B/205